THE INTERNATIONAL MARINE
SAILBOAT LIBRARY

TROUBLESHOOTING
MARINE DIESELS

PETER COMPTON

(www.boatdiesel.com)

INTERNATIONAL MARINE

CAMDEN, MAINE

This book is dedicated to
Penny,
the one ray of sunshine we can always count on.
Thanks for terrific daughters, Naomi and Kate, and 25 very special years.

And to
Rick Ramsdell,
a good friend and possibly the best diesel mechanic south of Alaska.

ACKNOWLEDGMENTS

The following engine and engine-component manufacturers helped me enormously in writing this book:

AB Volvo Penta
Alaska Diesel and Electric
Anchor Marine
Balmar, Inc.
Business Journals, Inc.
Caterpillar Engine Division
Cummins Engine Company, Ltd.
ITT Jabsco
Fleetguard, Inc.
Lister-Petter, Ltd.
Lucas, Ltd.
Pennzoil Products Company
Perkins International, Ltd.
R&D Couplings, Ltd.

Racor Division, Parker Hannifin
    Corporation
Robert Bosch Corporation
Velvet Drive Transmissions
Westerbeke Corporation
Yanmar Diesel America
    Corporation
Vulcan Couplings, Inc.
ZF Marine, Inc.

Local companies who assisted:

Tortola Marine Management
The Moorings
Freedom Yacht Charters
Tradewind Yachting Services

A very special thanks to the team at **Parts and Power, Ltd.**, Tortola, British Virgin Islands, whose support and first-class technical knowl-

CONTENTS

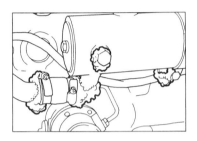

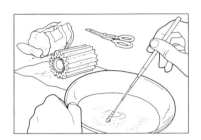

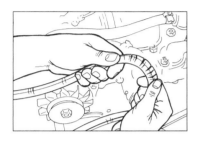

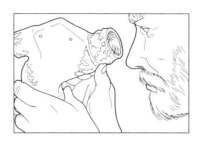

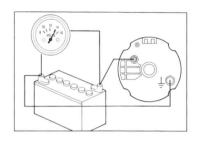

INTRODUCTION

"Knock! Knock!" says the owner as his head pops out of the engine bay.

"Who's there?" says I, playing the game.

"No! No! You bloody fool—the engine went 'knock knock,' then 'screech,' before it died!"

Down in the engine room, we find the crankshaft totally seized. The bilge is full of oil, and nothing shows on the dipstick. Thirty seconds later, we locate the culprit—the oil pipe to the engine-oil cooler had chafed through after months of rubbing against a rear engine mount. All the oil pumped into the bilge as the owner happily motored through the Virgin Islands. It probably happened so quickly that *anyone* would have been lucky to notice the drop in oil pressure on the gauge. Still, why didn't the low–oil-pressure switch set off the alarm bell? It finally comes out that there had been a short in the bell's wiring, and the owner disconnected the wires because the alarm was too noisy.

Like all such stories, this one has a moral. If only the owner had fixed the wiring short,

the alarm would have given him enough warning to shut down the engine before any serious damage occurred. A daily check on the engine might have spotted a drop in oil level on the dipstick or excess oil in the bilge. Certainly, a more thorough inspection would have picked up the chafed hose long before it failed. The consequences were expensive: a new engine, three weeks stuck in a marina waiting for the replacement to be shipped from the States, and another expensive week having it professionally installed.

The secret to a troublefree engine isn't knowing how to repair it, but knowing how to maintain it so you don't have to repair it.

This volume offers a detailed approach to diesel maintenance from the owner's point of view. It doesn't delve into theory or look at overhauls and repairs that require special skills, tools, manuals, or a workshop.

Determining the cause of a problem can be a mind-boggling task. In many cases, the symptoms lead straight to the obvious cause. More often,

6

though, a problem can stem from one of many faults and produce one or more symptoms. As in medicine, the diagnosis is not always straightforward. Frequently, there is insufficient evidence to confirm the cause at first glance; you may have to examine individual components or conduct further tests in a process of elimination.

The Troubleshooting Charts in Chapter 2, in combination with the System Fault Tables at the end of each chapter, cover most marine diesel problems and should make the diagnostic process easier.

The reality of diesel maintenance is far from the ideal workbench conditions most manuals show. Often you'll be hanging upside down, squeezed into an impossible position, trying to unscrew a drain plug you can feel only with the fingertips of your left hand. If you lose it, you know it's headed straight into the bilge. Space will always be at a premium in a sailboat, and difficult access can make it tempting to put off maintenance for another day. Make the effort—you'll

enjoy sailing much more knowing that the "Iron Genny" is always there when you need it.

If I've done my part well this book should soon be covered in oily fingerprints. It should save you big bucks—and probably put me out of a job.

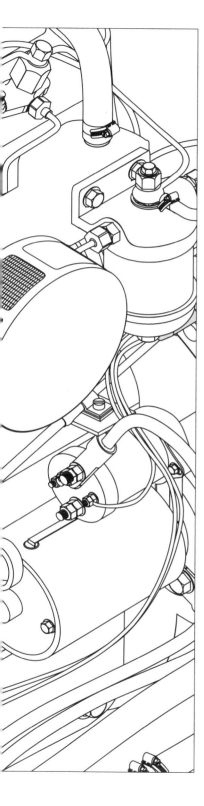

1
MAINTAINING YOUR DIESEL

MAINTENANCE TASK	FREQUENCY
Full System Inspection	seasonally
Mechanical System	
Check valve clearances	every 250* hours
Check cylinder head torque	after first 50 hours
Check engine alignment	every 250* hours
Oil System	
Check for leaks	daily
Check oil level	daily
Change oil	after first 50 hours & every 125* hours
Change oil filter	after first 50 hours & every 125* hours
Coolant Circuit	
Check coolant level	daily
Change coolant	every 250* hours
Check fan belt tension	daily
Raw-Water Circuit	
Check raw-water flow	daily
Check impeller	every 250* hours
Check heat exchangers & oil coolers	every 250* hours
Fuel System	
Check primary filter bowl	daily
Change primary fuel filter	every 125* hours
Change secondary fuel filter	every 250* hours
Test injectors	every 1,000 hours
Intake and Exhaust Systems	
Change paper and foam type intake filters	every 250* hours
Clean metal intake filters	every 250* hours
Electrical System	
Check battery fluid	after first 50 hours & every 125* hours
Transmissions	
Check fluid level	after first 50 hours & every 125* hours
Corrosion Protection	
Inspect and rectify as necessary	daily

* or seasonally, whichever comes first

A diesel engine, properly installed and maintained, will give thousands of hours of reliable service. Sadly, few marine diesels fitted to pleasure craft ever have the chance to wear out; poor maintenance condemns nearly all of them.

"If it ain't broke, don't fix it!" Like most sayings, this one contains an element of truth. Unfortunately, most boat owners—and quite a few professionals—treat it as gospel. How wrong they are!

Think safety for a moment. Visualize a so-called safe anchorage. A violent squall screams through in the wee hours, the wind veers, the hook trips, and suddenly the boat is beam-on, dragging toward concrete docks. You press the start button, but nothing happens.

Think money. Maintenance procedures are relatively inexpensive. Major repairs caused by poor maintenance are anything but.

Think time. Boating is about fun, relaxation, and leisure. A well-planned trip, whether it's a day sail, a weekend downriver, or that dream bluewater cruise, can quickly turn into an oily, stress-filled disaster, with more time spent stripping diesels than sipping sundowners.

"If it ain't broke, don't fix it" may appear to work in the short term, but each time you ignore your diesel, you notch up another IOU. One day you'll have to pay—big time.

A better maxim might be: "Look after your diesel and it will look after you." More than 99 percent of problems can be avoided with good maintenance. Whether you're mechanically minded or employ others to do the work, don't put yourself and your crew at risk with a poorly maintained, unreliable engine.

GOOD OPERATING PROCEDURE

A solid maintenance program includes operating a diesel within its designed limits:

- Keep the engine clean; layers of oil and dirt can hide many problems.
- Keep fuel clean and free of water.
- Keep engine free of corrosion.
- Inspect daily before starting.
- Check-start the engine well before departure.
- Allow the engine to reach operating temperature before heading out.
- Avoid prolonged idling.
- Avoid overloading the engine.
- Allow the engine to cool before shutting it down.

ROUTINE MAINTENANCE

Whether you call it routine, scheduled, or preventive maintenance, rare is the owner who habitually carries out the few tasks necessary to keep a diesel engine running reliably. Without regular trips to the engine bay, you miss the opportunity to look over the engine for unexpected problems and to correct them before they jeopardize your safety, time, and money.

Even an engine that is working well will slowly deteriorate with normal use. Regularly scheduled preventive maintenance tasks lessen the effects of such wear and tear before noticeably affecting performance and reliability. Inspect V-belts, fuel filters, and fluid levels daily. Take time to examine the engine for anything amiss. In addition to looking for loose and broken parts, check for leaks and belt dust—telltale signs of other problems. Always treat corrosion *before* it eats important and expensive components. Replace suspect hoses and clamps *before* they have a chance to fail. Follow your engine's maintenance schedule or, if you don't have a manual, follow the recommendations on page 9. Once every season, carry out a more thorough inspection of each engine system, as detailed in later chapters.

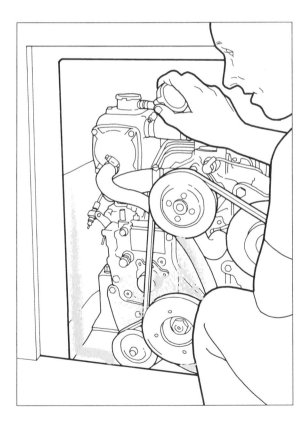

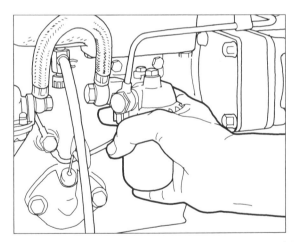

SURVEYING THE ENGINE: THE INITIAL INSPECTION

There are several occasions when you should survey the diesel's condition, even though it appears to be running well. Whether you're buying or selling a boat, getting ready for that once-in-a-lifetime bluewater cruise, or simply preparing for the coming season, performing a thorough engine survey will reduce the chances of an unexpected failure, and boost your peace of mind every time you need the diesel.

THE VISUAL INSPECTION

The engine compartment's general condition can indicate how well the diesel has been maintained. A clean, neatly painted engine suggests good care. On the other hand, a few layers of paint can hide a multitude of problems. Look in those awkward places where a brush or spray couldn't reach.

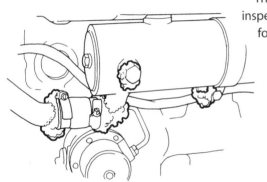

The following table lists each engine system and the items to inspect. The cross-reference column points to more detailed information elsewhere in the book.

Run methodically through each of these tasks, and you'll cover more than most mechanics do during a full engine survey.

COMPONENT	CHECK FOR	PAGE
Mechanical System (Chapter 3)		
Engine block	loose components, cracks, corrosion	—
Crankshaft	free rotation	26
Freeze plugs	leaks, corrosion	49
Cylinder-head gasket	leaks	50
Engine mounts	loose nuts, corrosion	54
Engine alignment	easy shaft rotation	55
Oil System (Chapter 4)		
System	external oil leaks	63
Oil	correct level, condition of oil, contamination	61
Oil cooler	leaks, corrosion	85

COMPONENT	CHECK FOR	PAGE
Raw-Water Circuit (Chapter 5)		
Through-hull fitting and valve	operation, leaks, corrosion	78
Raw-water strainer	debris, corrosion, leaks	78
Hoses, pipes, and clamps	deterioration, chafe, corrosion, tightness	90
Raw-water pump	external leaks, corrosion	79
Heat exchangers	external corrosion, leaks	85
Antisiphon valve	operation	89
Sacrificial anodes or "zincs"	condition	87
Coolant Circuit (Chapter 6)		
Coolant	level, condition	95
Pressure cap	good sealing, correct pressure rating	99
Expansion tank	level, coolant condition	99
V-belt	correct tension, condition	102
Circulating pump	bearing play, seal leakage	101
Header tank	leaks, corrosion, loose fittings	99
Fuel System (Chapter 7)		
Fuel tanks	fillers, vents, fittings, valves, hoses	109
Primary filter	water, dirt, algae growth	110
Lift pump	leaks, external corrosion	111
Secondary filter	external fuel leaks	113
injector pump	attachment to block, external leaks	115
Injector pipes	leaks, good support, corrosion	—
Intake and Exhaust System (Chapter 8)		
Intake filter	cleanliness	130
Exhaust manifold	loose fittings, leaks, corrosion	131
Exhaust injection elbow	raw-water and exhaust gas leakage, loose attachment, internal restrictions	131
Exhaust hose and clamps	deterioration, corrosion	132
Lift box/muffler	corrosion, splitting, leaks	133
Turbocharger	cleanliness, free rotation	134
Intercooler	corrosion, external leakage	135
Electrical System (Chapter 9)		
Batteries	electrolyte level and specific gravity, voltage, condition of plates and casing	139
Battery switches	connections, corrosion	144
Starter	connections, corrosion	148
Alternator	connections, corrosion	145
Battery isolation diodes	connections, corrosion	—
Wiring	loose wiring, chafing, loose or corroded connections, burned or melted insulation	—
Controls and Instruments (Chapter 10)		
Throttle control	smooth operation, full travel	153
Gear-selector controls	smooth operation, full travel	155
Mechanical stop control	smooth operation, full travel	156
Electrical stop control	loose connections, corrosion	156
Control cables	smooth operation, external corrosion	157
Gauges	water temperature and oil pressure should zero when the ignition is switched on	159

SURVEYING THE ENGINE: THE STARTUP

You can't properly survey an engine without running it. If the boat is out of the water, run a water supply into a bucket with a separate hose connected to the raw-water pump inlet. Running the engine out of the water will not cover all the following checks, but it will give a good indication of engine condition.

Before you start the engine, check:

Throttle mechanism. Check for full and free throttle travel from stop to stop. Be sure to return the throttle arm to the idle stop.

Cable stop mechanism. Check for full and free travel. Ensure the lever returns to the run position.

Solenoid stop mechanism. Check that the wiring is good. In particular, push on connectors that often vibrate loose.

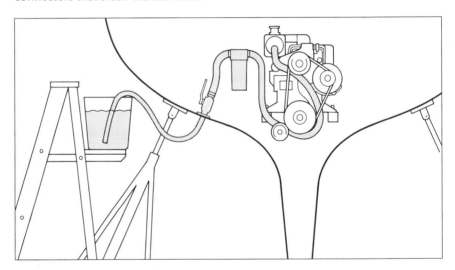

Start the engine and check:

Quick Start. A good engine should start instantly, without needing several turns of the crankshaft. Cold-weather starting will take a little longer, since cold metal absorbs heat from the compressed air. If the engine starts slowly, shut it off and start it again. This time it should start immediately. Instant starting confirms that the compression, fuel delivery and atomization, battery, and starter are good. Avoid using starting fluid. If a diesel will not start without starting fluid, it needs repair. If the engine will not start or proves difficult to start, follow the Troubleshooting Charts in Chapter 2.

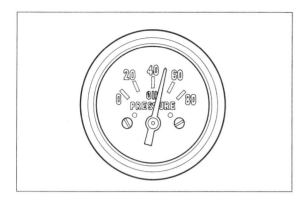

Oil Pressure. If the gauge doesn't register oil pressure within 15 seconds of starting, shut down the engine. Pressures vary among engines, and will be higher when the engine is cold. Consistently low oil pressure suggests a worn engine. (Troubleshooting Chart 4)

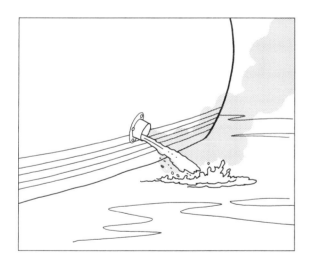

Exhaust Smoke. Modern, environmentally friendly engines produce little smoke, but older engines—even those in good condition—may produce light smoke. It is normal to see smoke during and immediately after starting, but it should clear to almost nothing within the first few minutes. (Troubleshooting Chart 5)

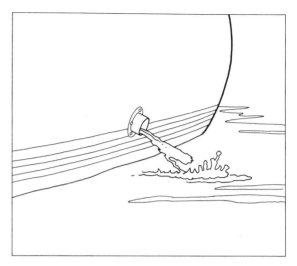

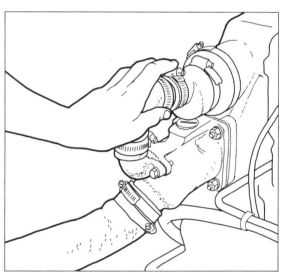

Raw-Water Circulation. Check that plenty of raw water is coming out of the exhaust outlet (top). The raw-water pipe feeding the exhaust injection elbow should feel warm, not hot or cold (above). (Chapter 8)

Noise and Vibration. With the engine running, listen and feel for anything abnormal. (Troubleshooting Chart 7)

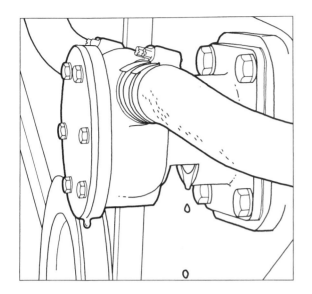

Leaks. Look for oil, coolant, and raw-water leaks. Check for fuel leaks around the injectors. Soot deposits in this area indicate poor gas sealing of the copper seat washers.

Water Temperature. Allow the engine temperature to stabilize, and check that it is close to the thermostat rating. There should be little fluctuation. (Troubleshooting Chart 6)

Charging. Check the alternator output. The charging light should go out immediately after startup, although some installations require rpm to be increased above idle. An ammeter fitted in the circuit will show output as soon as the alternator starts charging. Standard alternators will initially charge at a high rate, but decrease rapidly as battery voltage increases. Voltage regulators typically control voltage at 14 to 14.5 volts. Measure voltage between the alternator's positive output terminal and casing ground to confirm output. (Troubleshooting Chart 9)

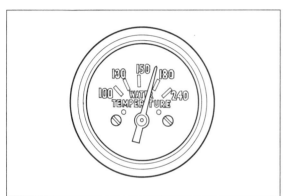

Transmission. Check for positive engagement in both forward and reverse.

No-Load RPM. If a tachometer is fitted, briefly push the throttle to maximum and check the rpm.

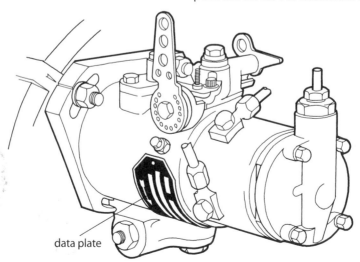

data plate

The engine should be within 10% of its rated rpm, which is usually stamped on the injector-pump data plate or can be listed in the engine specifications. Failure to reach rated no-load rpm could be due to a faulty tachometer, but more often suggests other problems. (Troubleshooting Chart 3)

SURVEYING THE ENGINE: THE SEA TRIAL

Take the boat out to a clear stretch of calm water and operate the engine at gradually increasing rpm. Visually inspect the engine while it is under load, and look for leaks and vibrating components. Note the oil pressure, water temperature, and any exhaust smoke.

Check Maximum Achievable RPM. Most small engine manufacturers define a **maximum intermittent rating** for their engines. Theoretically, with a correctly matched transmission and propeller, an engine should reach this rating at the same time as a displacement vessel reaches hull speed. Provided the engine is normally operated below 90% of this rpm, the engine should not be overloaded and will still have a little in reserve when needed. Cruising sailors and certainly commercial operators looking for maximum service from an engine should match the transmission and propeller to the manufacturer's **maximum continuous rating.** (Troubleshooting Chart 3)

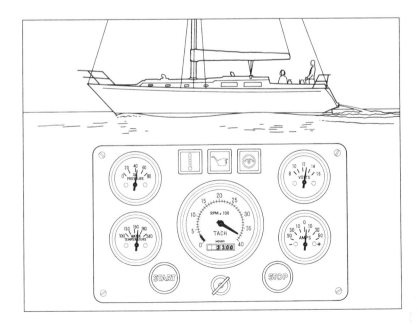

PREVENTING CORROSION

Corrosion is the natural deterioration of metals, due mostly to their surface reaction with oxygen. This reaction usually is chemical or electrochemical and is accelerated by the presence of water and heat. Electrochemical or electrolytic corrosion occurs through a reaction between dissimilar metals in the presence of water or chemicals that form an electrolyte.

Considering the combination of hot metal, hot exhaust gases, and sea-water to which they're exposed, it's not surprising that most engines head for the diesel graveyard long before they wear out. Corrosion is the marine diesel's number one enemy. During the life of the average diesel, owners will spend more money on corrosion-induced failures than any other cause.

Tell-tale signs of corrosion are:

Iron and steel: Brown or black staining, dust, or flakes.
Stainless steel: Black spots usually in areas starved of oxygen.
Aluminum: White powder or crystals of aluminum chloride.
Bronze, brass, and copper: Green staining or powder. Severe corrosion will
  dezincify base metal, leaving a copper-colored light pink.

With minimal forethought and regular maintenance, you can avoid nearly all corrosion problems. Just follow the two cardinal rules: Prevent water and chemicals from contacting bare metal; and keep dissimilar metals apart.

PAINT

The simplest way to protect metal surfaces is with a good layer of paint—a common practice with marine engines. Unfortunately, normal wear and tear and routine maintenance take a toll on paint finishes, exposing bare metal that will corrode rapidly. Don't rely on paint coverage alone.

CORROSION INHIBITORS

For additional protection, spray on a soft, protective, water-repellent layer of oils or waxes. There are several brands of inhibitors. Thinner oils provide good coverage for short-term protection; they're easy to apply and remove and are best suited to spotless engines with good paint coverage and no corrosion.

Thicker, heavy-duty corrosion inhibitors provide much more durable protection and can even be applied over corroded components. Good inhibitors remain soft and flexible but have the disadvantage of collecting dirt over time.

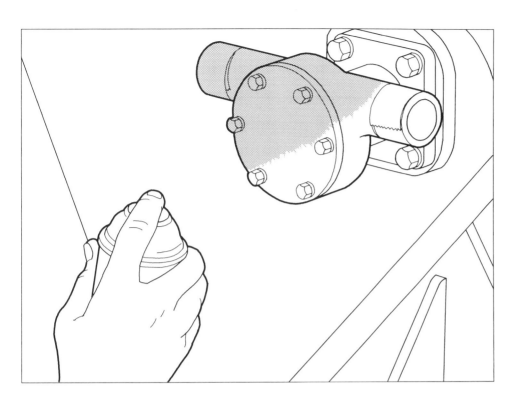

LAYING UP OR "WINTERIZING" A DIESEL

This procedure protects the engine inside and out against the elements and should be carried out whenever the engine will not be used for an extended period. The following steps are fairly standard regardless of climate:

1. Drain the coolant, opening all engine, heat-exchanger, and oil-cooler drains.
2. Replace the coolant with a clean, fresh, 50/50 mixture of water and antifreeze.
3. Replace the oil and oil filter. Normal combustion produces corrosive acids that are absorbed by the oil. Leaving dirty oil in the engine for an extended time allows these acids to attack and damage bearing surfaces.
4. Replace the fuel filter elements—draining any water from the filter bowls.
5. Bleed the fuel system of air.
6. Run the engine up to operating temperature.
7. Top off coolant and oil.
8. Close the raw-water inlet seacock.
9. Remove the raw-water pump impeller.
10. Backflush the raw-water circuit to remove corrosive salts by connecting a freshwater supply to the raw-water hose that feeds the exhaust injection elbow.
11. Drain the raw-water circuit thoroughly.
12. Fully charge the batteries. Disconnect all leads. Unattended, a battery naturally discharges over a period of several weeks. The electrolyte on a discharged battery can freeze at 20°F (-7°C), so keep the batteries fully charged or, better still, remove them to a warmer storage area. Small automatic trickle chargers work well.
13. Treat battery and cable terminals with petroleum jelly, silicone grease, or a heavy-duty corrosion inhibitor.
14. Protect external surfaces with a heavy-duty corrosion inhibitor.
15. Cover the engine with a waterproof sheet in case there are any leaks from above.

Points to remember:

- Filling the raw-water circuit with antifreeze will swell raw-water pump impellers and render them useless. Remove the impeller first if you are using antifreeze.
- Each time you visit the boat, additional protection can be achieved using the starter to turn the engine over and circulate oil to the bearings and cylinder walls. Remember to pull out the stop cable and keep turning until the low oil pressure light extinguishes or pressure registers on the gauge.

- Special inhibiting oils are available that provide greater protection. Use these to replace the standard engine oil; run the engine briefly to coat all surfaces, and then drain the oil. Protection remains good, provided the engine is not turned.
- If the engine cannot be fully winterized, replace oil, coolant, and all filters and run the engine up to operating temperatures monthly if possible.

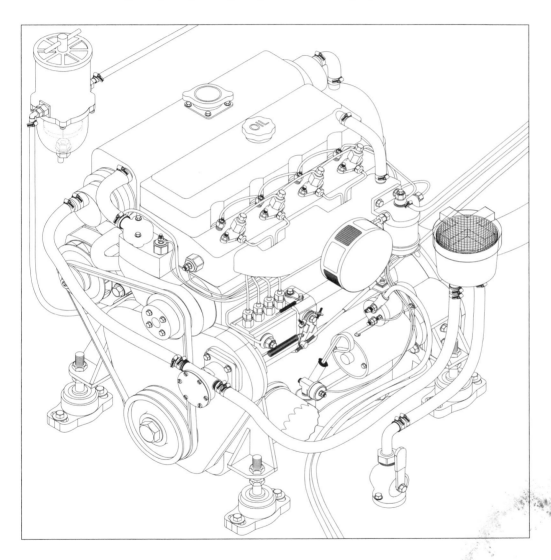

2
TROUBLESHOOTING MARINE DIESELS

Troubleshooting a sick diesel calls heavily on experience, a thorough knowledge of diesel operating principles, and most of all, the ability to think logically. Don't worry if you're missing the first two: that's where the troubleshooting charts below come in. Organize your thoughts as follows:

IDENTIFY THE SYMPTOMS

Ask yourself these few simple questions to get started.

❑ Did the problem occur suddenly or did it gradually worsen? Sudden problems are usually due to a blockage or component failure. Gradual worsening is most often caused by wear or slow degradation from contamination, corrosion, or dirt.

❑ Has anyone worked on the engine recently? Many problems are maintenance induced; perhaps a part was reassembled incorrectly.

❑ Was there excess smoke? Color and quantity of exhaust smoke is a helpful indicator. (See Chart 5.)

❑ Were there any unusual noises? Noise will often lead you to the problem, but keep an open mind: Noise in one area can be caused by a problem elsewhere. (See Chart 7.)

❑ Was there any unusual vibration? Same as above.

❑ What was the rpm doing? A sudden racing, slowing, or dying means something. (See Chart 3.)

❑ Has the engine lost power? (See Chart 3.)

❑ Was the oil pressure normal? Loss of oil pressure can lead to serious mechanical problems. (See Chart 4.)

❑ Was the water temperature normal? (See Chart 6.)

❑ Did the alarm sound? Low oil pressure or high water temperature trigger the alarm circuit. (See Charts 4 and 6.)

❑ Will the engine restart? (See Chart 1.)

USING THE TROUBLESHOOTING CHARTS AND SYSTEM FAULT TABLES THROUGHOUT THIS BOOK

❑ The Troubleshooting Charts in this chapter are simple flow diagrams that lead from symptoms to a list of possible causes.

❑ The Fault Tables at the end of the system chapters look at each component and list its common modes of failure, causes, and possible symptoms.

Approach the charts and tables with common sense and treat them purely as tools to guide you in the right direction. They were compiled primarily for four-stroke, water-cooled diesels and cover the majority of problems you may encounter with these engines. Nevertheless, owners of air-cooled or two-stroke diesels should also find the charts valuable.

REMEMBER THE "HOW LIKELY" FACTOR

Use the following probability factors as a general guide in the Troubleshooting Charts and the System Fault Tables. Direct your initial investigation toward faults with a factor of 1, 2, or 3, until additional information points you elsewhere.

[1]	Very Common	Occurs very frequently; check this first.
[2]	Common	Occurs fairly frequently.
[3]	Possible	Does not occur too often.
[4]	Rare	May never occur in the life of the average diesel.
[5]	Very Rare	Theoretically possible, but few mechanics will ever see it. Don't waste too much time exploring this possibility unless you've tried everything else.

CHART 1

TROUBLESHOOTING MARINE DIESELS—START HERE

Diesel engine problems, at their most basic, usually fall into one of three categories: engine fails to start, engine not running correctly, or engine fails to stop. More specific symptoms flow from these three options. Always start here when troubleshooting a problem with your diesel.

ENGINE FAILS TO START

ENGINE DOES NOT TURN

1. **Confirm the engine turns over freely.** GO TO **CHART 2**

2. **Confirm the starting system is working correctly.** GO TO **CHART 8**

ENGINE TURNS SLOWLY

1. **Is the oil viscosity correct? Too heavy an oil will make the engine difficult to turn over, especially in cold weather.** GO TO **Chapter 4**

2. **Confirm the engine will turn over freely.** GO TO **CHART 2**

3. **Confirm the starting system is working correctly.** GO TO **CHART 8**

ENGINE TURNS NORMALLY— BUT FAILS TO START

1. **Check fuel is reaching the injectors.** GO TO **CHART 11**

2. **Check the intake and exhaust systems for restrictions.** GO TO **Chapter 8**

3. **Check for good compression.** GO TO **Chapter 4**

4. **If you have not found a fault at this stage then your problems are becoming more serious. Before you take further action recheck the above systems thoroughly.**

ENGINE NOT RUNNING CORRECTLY

PERFORMANCE PROBLEMS → GO TO **CHART 3**

STARTING SYSTEM PROBLEMS → GO TO **CHART 8**

OIL PROBLEMS → GO TO **CHART 4**

CHARGING SYSTEM PROBLEMS → GO TO **CHART 9**

SMOKE PROBLEMS → GO TO **CHART 5**

TURBOCHARGER PROBLEMS → GO TO **CHART 10**

TEMPERATURE PROBLEMS → GO TO **CHART 6**

FUEL PROBLEMS → GO TO **CHART 11**

NOISE AND VIBRATION PROBLEMS → GO TO **CHART 7**

SHUT DOWN → GO TO **CHART 12**

ENGINE FAILS TO STOP

 GO TO **CHART 12**

CHART 2

CHECK CRANKSHAFT TURNS FREELY

If you suspect a mechanical problem, turning the engine over slowly by hand will allow you to feel any abnormal resistance. Use a wrench on a convenient crankshaft bolt to turn the engine in its normal direction of rotation—clockwise when viewed from the front. If no crankshaft bolt is accessible, use the alternator pulley nut and apply pressure to the middle of the belt to stop slipping. You must turn the crankshaft of a four-stroke engine at least two full turns before you can be sure the pistons are not hitting anything they shouldn't!

NO MOVEMENT

A. Engine stopped suddenly
Probably due to overheating or lack of lubrication.

CAUSES:

- ❑ Piston seized in cylinder [3]
- ❑ Main bearings seized [4]
- ❑ Rod bearings seized [4]

B. Engine ran well when last used
Probably caused by corrosion.

CAUSES:

- ❑ Raw water in the cylinder head [2]
- ❑ Starter seized with the gear engaged [4]

TURNS SLIGHTLY IN EACH DIRECTION

Slight movement in both directions suggests the crankshaft is able to move but a component attached to the timing gears is broken or seized.

CAUSES:

- ❑ Gear box seized [3]
- ❑ Gear-driven pump seized [4]
- ❑ Timing gears jammed or seized [4]
- ❑ Camshaft followers seized [4]
- ❑ Camshaft seized [5]

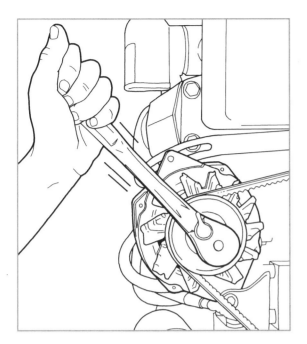

TIGHT AND DIFFICULT TO TURN

Before you strip the engine, remember that as each piston reaches the top of its compression stroke, considerably more effort is required to turn the engine over. This is normal. If you are not sure that compression is the reason it's tight, remove the injectors and turn the engine over again.

CAUSES:

❑ Normal compression   [2]
❑ Gearbox still selected   [2]
❑ Piston rings/cylinders scuffing   [4]
❑ Bearings binding   [4]
❑ Starter gear jammed in flywheel ring gear   [4]

TURNS BUT LOCKS UP IN BOTH DIRECTIONS

Easy movement during crankshaft rotation that stops solidly suggests a reciprocating component is broken or locking up. Before stripping the engine, remove the injectors to check for fluid—particularly water—in the cylinder.

CAUSES:

❑ Water, coolant, oil, or fuel in cylinder   [2]
❑ Connecting rod broken   [4]
❑ Valve dropped into cylinder   [4]
❑ Cam followers seized   [4]
❑ Crankshaft broken   [5]

CHART
3

PERFORMANCE PROBLEMS

A change in performance can be sudden or gradual. It covers everything from a slight drop in maximum rpm to the engine dying unexpectedly. Remember the basic rules: Sudden change suggests a defect or failure; gradual change suggests degradation from wear or contamination.

LOSS OF POWER

Check no-load rpm first—see Chapter 1.

If rpm is within 10% of governor setting, most likely cause of power loss is overloading. If rpm fails to get within 10% of setting, check fuel, air, and compression.

CAUSES:

A. Overloading (expect dark exhaust smoke)
- Propeller dirty [1]
- Boat bottom dirty [1]
- Transmission or prop shaft binding [2]
- Incorrect propeller [3]
- Incorrect transmission ratio [3]

B. Poor fuel supply
- Injector defective [1]
- Air in fuel system [1]
- Fuel filter contaminated [2]
- Water in fuel [2]
- Control cable travel restricted [3]
- Two sealing washers under injector [3]
- Injector pipes leaking [3]
- Lift pump defective [4]
- Injector pump contaminated [4]
- Fuel tank vent restricted [4]
- Governor sticking [4]
- Fuel grade incorrect [4]
- Incorrect timing [4]

C. Restricted air supply (expect dark exhaust smoke)
- Restricted air intake [2]
- Restricted exhaust [3]

D. Compression low
- Valve clearances incorrect [3]
- Valve seats worn [3]
- Piston rings worn or broken and cylinders worn [3]

E. Oil system
- Incorrect oil grade [4]

ENGINE DIES

Common cause is restricted primary filter. If so, engine usually restarts if left for a few minutes while the fuel filters through, but will shut down soon after.

CAUSES:

A. Restricted fuel supply
- Air in fuel system [1]
- Fuel filter clogged [1]
- Water in fuel [2]
- Fuel tank empty [3]
- Fuel tank vent restricted [3]
- Lift pump defective [4]
- Governor failure [5]

B. Mechanical problems

- ❑ Engine seized [3]
- ❑ Debris around prop or shaft [2]
- ❑ Transmission seized [4]

ACCELERATION POOR

Poor acceleration is closely allied to loss of power, so check the problems under "Loss of Power" first.

CAUSES:

If the engine produces good power but acceleration is slow then it is possible that the acceleration limiter on the governor mechanism is incorrectly set. Not all governors have an acceleration-limiter adjustment, and those that do are usually factory set. Leave any adjustment to the experts.

MISFIRING OR SURGING

Misfiring or surging where engine rpm is erratic or the engine does not appear to be firing on all cylinders is mostly caused by inconsistent fuel supply.

CAUSES:

A. Erratic fuel delivery

- ❑ Injector(s) defective [1]
- ❑ Fuel filter clogged [2]

- ❑ Air in fuel system [2]
- ❑ Water in fuel [3]
- ❑ Injection timing incorrect [4]
- ❑ Governor linkage sticking [4]
- ❑ Governor defective [4]

B. Erratic compression

- ❑ Intake or exhaust valve sticking [4]

DECELERATION POOR

When the throttle setting is decreased, engine maintains rpm or is slow to decelerate.

CAUSES:

- ❑ Throttle-lever return spring tired or broken [3]
- ❑ Fuel rack sticking [4]

IDLE RPM INCORRECT

Idle rpm adjustment is the only setting on the fuel pump or governor that may be adjusted. When the idle rpm requires adjustment, it usually indicates a problem elsewhere. Make adjustments only when the engine is warm and working properly!

MAXIMUM RPM INCORRECT

Maximum rpm is factory set and should not be adjusted.

A. Maximum rpm high

CAUSES:

- ❑ Injector pump out of adjustment [4]
- ❑ Governor weights broken [5]

B. Maximum rpm low

- ❑ Follow procedure for loss of power, above.

CHART

4

OIL PROBLEMS

A loss of oil pressure will seize the engine within seconds. Never run the engine if the oil system is suspect. If you don't have an oil gauge, consider installing one.

OIL CONTAMINATION

Oil contamination is covered in Chapter 4. Any contamination must be removed quickly, the cause rectified, and the system cleaned before you run the engine again.

A. Coolant in Oil

If the engine has recently been run, the oil and coolant will emulsify and appear milky. Left to settle, the water will have the same coloring as the engine coolant. Do not be fooled by clear water droplets on the oil filler cap—these are from condensed vapor that can originate from coolant, raw water, or natural condensation.

CAUSES:

❑ Coolant poured into oil filler	[2]
❑ Cylinder-head gasket failed	[3]
❑ Cylinder head cracked	[4]
❑ Engine block cracked	[4]
❑ Cylinder liner cracked	[4]
❑ Liner seals defective	[4]
❑ Cracked exhaust manifold	[4]

B. Raw water

If the engine has recently been run, the oil and raw water will emulsify and appear milky. Left to settle, the water should appear clear. Often, saltwater crystals on the dipstick or components will help identification. Do not be fooled by clear water droplets on the oil filler cap—these are from condensed vapor that can originate from coolant, raw water, or natural condensation.

CAUSES:

❑ Gear-driven raw-water pumps—seal failure or in-adequate greasing on old style with solid body	[2]
❑ Antisiphon valve stuck closed	[2]
❑ Exhaust system—poor design	[2]
❑ Engine oil cooler failed	[3]
❑ Cylinder-head gasket failed—direct-cooled engines	[3]
❑ Intercooler failed (if fitted)	[3]
❑ Cracked exhaust manifold	[4]

C. Fuel

Level may rise on dipstick. Oil will appear thin with a strong smell of diesel.

CAUSES:

❑ Lift pump diaphragm	[4]
❑ Injector pump seals	[4]

D. Metal

If metal is visible in the oil when drained, much more is in the bottom of the oil pan. Cut open the used oil-filter cartridge and remove the oil pan. Depending on the quantity, the problems could be very serious and mean a full engine strip. If you catch the cause early enough, you may save the engine. Can be almost any component whose bearing surface is lubricated by the oil system.

CAUSES:

❑ Piston rings/cylinders	[3]
❑ Main bearings	[4]
❑ Rod bearings	[4]
❑ Valve gear	[4]
❑ Timing gears	[5]
❑ Oil pump	[5]

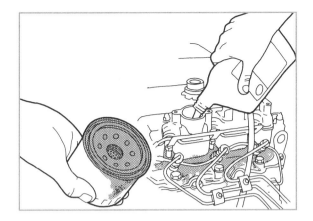

E. Oil dirty and black

If the oil is thin, dirty, and black, it is probably heavily contaminated with combustion products. Modern quality oils contain dispersants that prevent the contamination from forming a sludge.

CAUSES:

❑ Infrequent oil changes [1]
❑ Excessive combustion products [2]

OIL PRESSURE INCORRECT

A. High oil pressure

Oil consumption and blue exhaust smoke may increase with the denser crankcase oil mist. This is neither common nor a serious problem.

CAUSES:

❑ Defective gauge [3]
❑ Pump pressure-relief valve sticking closed [3]
❑ Incorrect grade of oil [4]

B. Low oil pressure

Low pressure can have serious consequences—always investigate.

CAUSES:

❑ Oil level low [1]
❑ Oil filter restricted [2]
❑ Oil temperature too high [2]

❑ Excessive wear on bearings [3]
❑ Defective gauge [3]
❑ Oil viscosity too low [4]
❑ Oil pump worn [4]
❑ Pressure-relief valve relieving low [4]
❑ Oil pump pickup tube defective [5]

EXTERNAL OIL LEAKS

To locate leaks, clean the engine first and then run at fast idle while looking for the source. A clean piece of paper or absorbent sheet under the engine will make leaks more apparent.

CAUSES:

❑ Valve-cover gasket [2]
❑ Flywheel seal [3]
❑ Crankshaft seal [3]
❑ Oil-pan gasket [3]
❑ Timing-cover gasket [3]
❑ External pipes connecting oil cooler [3]
❑ Oil in exhaust water—failed oil cooler [3]
❑ Lift pump gasket or pivot [3]

HIGH OIL CONSUMPTION

All engines burn oil to some extent. On new engines, the amount is not normally enough that oil has to be added between oil changes. As the engine starts to wear, expect to add oil occasionally. High oil consumption is not seriously detrimental to the engine provided the level is maintained.

CAUSES:

❑ External leaks [2]
❑ Cylinders/piston rings worn [3]
❑ Valve guides worn [3]
❑ Valve seals worn [3]
❑ Excessive oil [3]
❑ Incorrect oil grade [4]
❑ Engine-oil cooler leaking internally [4]

CHART 5

EXCESSIVE EXHAUST SMOKE

The color and quantity of exhaust smoke tells a great deal about the condition of a diesel. Most engines create some smoke, but if the diesel is in good condition the quantity will be almost invisible. Defects that affect the fuel, breathing, or compression will prevent correct combustion and lead to excessive exhaust smoke.

WHITE SMOKE

White exhaust smoke is unburned fuel that can be caused by excessive fuel or poor combustion.

CAUSES:

A. Poor atomization
❑ Injector nozzle stuck open   [1]
❑ Injector-nozzle seat worn   [1]
❑ Injector pressure low   [1]
❑ Low ambient temperature   [3]
❑ Low fuel grade   [4]
❑ Injection timing retarded   [4]

B. Poor compression
❑ Leaking inlet or exhaust valves   [3]
❑ Worn piston rings and cylinders   [3]
❑ Piston rings stuck in grooves   [3]

C. Water in fuel
Small quantities of water in the fuel will show as white exhaust smoke.

❑ Contaminated fuel   [2]
❑ Defective cylinder-head gasket   [3]

Note: Excessive periods at idle cause a buildup of unburned fuel within the exhaust system that burns off in the first few minutes the next time the engine is operated under normal power. This condition is normal for diesel engines and common in sailboats that idle for lengthy periods charging batteries or running freezers.

HOW LIKELY?   [1] Very common   [2] Common   [3] Possible   [4] Rare   [5] Very rare

BLACK OR DARK SMOKE

Black smoke is caused by partially burned fuel. When the fuel/air mixture increases there is insufficient oxygen in the cylinders to complete combustion. Large quantities of carbon appear from the exhaust as minute, black soot particles.

CAUSES:

A. Engine overloaded

As load increases on the engine, the governor senses the slight decrease in rpm and adjusts the injector pump to deliver more fuel. If the engine becomes overloaded, the increase in fuel does not increase rpm and no extra air is sucked into the cylinders. Net result: soot.

☐ Propeller dirty or fouled [1]
☐ Boat bottom dirty [1]
☐ Engine alignment incorrect [2]
☐ Transmission ratio incorrect [3]
☐ Propeller incorrect [3]

B. Insufficient air

☐ Air-intake filter clogged [2]
☐ Air intake restricted [3]
☐ Exhaust restricted [3]
☐ Leaking inlet or exhaust valves [4]
☐ Poor engine room ventilation [4]

C. Excessive fuel

☐ Defective injector(s) [1]
☐ Incorrect injector nozzle [3]
☐ Two sealing washers under injector [3]
☐ Injector pump incorrectly set [4]
☐ Low fuel grade [4]

STEAM

If you are not sure whether the white cloud from the exhaust is smoke or steam, watch how it dissipates. Steam or water vapor will rise and clear fairly quickly. Smoke tends to stay closer to the water and take longer to dilute with the local breezes.

CAUSES:

☐ Water vapor from condensing exhaust gases is normal in colder climates [1]
☐ Insufficient raw-water flow [2]
☐ Excessive exhaust-gas temperatures [4]

BLUE SMOKE

More accurately, the smoke will appear white with a hint of blue. It often takes a trained eye to differentiate.

CAUSES:

☐ Valve seals defective [3]
☐ Valve guides worn [3]
☐ Piston rings/cylinders worn [3]
☐ High crankcase pressure [3]
☐ Oil leaking into the intake from defective gaskets [4]

CHART
6

TEMPERATURE PROBLEMS

If your engine overheats, shut it down before any damage occurs. Running an engine at too high a temperature will cause severe damage in a very short time. Temperatures above 220°F (105°C) reduce the lubrication properties of the oil, and components will begin to fail. Always let the engine cool naturally. It may take several hours before the engine can be worked on. Be patient!

Never remove the filler cap or add cold water until the engine has cooled.

TEMPERATURE HIGH

Can mean a gradual degradation of the system caused by wear or a buildup of salts, marine growth, or corrosion. Sudden increases are caused by component failure or system blockage. A common cause, which can be difficult to diagnose, is a plastic bag or similar debris covering the raw-water inlet. Suction holds the bag in place while the engine is running, but as soon as it is shut down the bag disappears. In the meantime, the lack of water has probably destroyed the raw-water pump impeller.

ENGINES WITH FRESH-WATER COOLING
A. Insufficient raw water
❏ Raw-water impeller defective [1]
❏ Restriction in raw-water inlet or strainer [1]
❏ Heat exchanger dirty [2]
❏ Oil cooler dirty [2]
❏ Exhaust injection elbow restricted [3]
❏ Leaking hose/filter gaskets before raw-water pump letting air into system (if above waterline) [3]
❏ Raw-water pump cam worn [3]
❏ Exhaust manifold restricted [4]

B. Insufficient coolant circulation

- ❏ Coolant level low   [2]
- ❏ V-belt broken or slipping   [2]
- ❏ Thermostat sticking closed   [2]
- ❏ Coolant circuit dirty or restricted   [2]

Note: Engines that incorporate a "by-pass" circuit in the cooling system will overheat if the thermostat sticks open or is removed.

ENGINES WITH RAW-WATER COOLING
A. Insufficient raw water

- ❏ Raw-water inlet or strainer blocked   [1]
- ❏ Raw-water impeller defective   [1]
- ❏ Thermostat stuck closed   [2]
- ❏ Exhaust injection manifold restricted   [2]
- ❏ Cylinder block dirty or restricted   [3]
- ❏ Exhaust manifold waterways restricted   [4]

ALL ENGINES
A. Inadequate lubrication

- ❏ Insufficient oil   [3]
- ❏ Contaminated oil   [3]

B. Engine generating excessive heat

- ❏ Fuel problems   [2]
- ❏ Overloading   [3]

C. False indication

- ❏ Defective gauge or sender   [4]

TEMPERATURE LOW

Engines with indirect cooling systems operate at 160–195°F (70–90°C). Direct-cooled engines operate at much lower temperatures: 120–140°F (50–60°C). An engine running at low temperatures will have reduced life due to buildup of acids on the cylinder wall, which cause wear. Both indirect and direct systems use a thermostat to control temperature. Low temperatures are nearly always due to problems with the thermostat.

CAUSES:

- ❏ Thermostat stuck open   [2]
- ❏ No thermostat fitted   [2]
- ❏ Incorrect thermostat   [4]
- ❏ Very low ambient temperatures   [4]

TEMPERATURE ERRATIC

The temperature gauge will fluctuate as though it is sticking. Temperatures will be higher and lower than normal.

CAUSES:

- ❏ Thermostat sticking   [2]
- ❏ False indication   [4]

CHART 7

NOISE AND VIBRATION PROBLEMS

Engine noise and vibration are excellent indicators of the onset of a problem. Although these symptoms are difficult to quantify, most owners hear or feel a change in the engine the second it occurs. Even if your experience is limited, trust these senses and investigate further.

If you're having trouble locating the source of a noise or vibration, try using a large screwdriver as a stethoscope by placing the sharp end on different parts of the engine and the rounded handle hard against your ear. A piece of wood can be equally effective.

NOISE

A. Knocking
Sounds like: Hammer hitting engine block. Hard mechanical sound with frequency proportional to engine rpm.

CAUSES:

❑ Defective injector [2]
❑ Excessive fuel [3]
❑ Worn connecting-rod bearing [4]
❑ Connecting-rod bolt loose [4]
❑ Piston hitting valve [4]
❑ Injection timing too far advanced [4]
❑ Flywheel loose [5]

B. Rattling
Sounds like: One or a handful of nuts being shaken in an empty metal can.

CAUSES:

❑ Excessive valve clearances [2]
❑ Loose accessories [2]

C. Rumbling
Sounds like: Slow-speed, dull sound, like assorted rocks being turned in a large drum.

CAUSES:

❑ Propeller shaft out of balance [2]
❑ Cutlass bearing worn [2]
❑ Propeller out of balance [2]
❑ Gearbox bearings worn [4]
❑ Drive plate worn or loose [4]

D. Squealing
Sounds like: Car tires during a racing start.

CAUSES:

❑ Fan belt slipping [1]
❑ Lack of lubrication on piston [3]
❑ Gasoline in fuel tank [5]

E. Hissing air
Sounds like: Escaping gas. Occurs intermittently as a piston approaches the top of its compression stroke.

CAUSES:

❑ Leaking injector seating washer [2]
❑ Leaking cylinder-head gasket [3]
❑ Leaking inlet-valve seat [4]

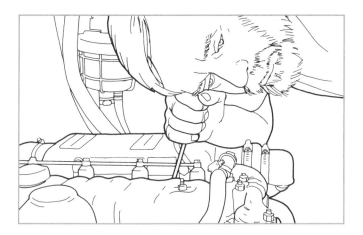

F. Clicking

Sounds like: Light metallic sound that can occur once or continuously.

CAUSES:

❏ Starter solenoid engaging—once is normal [2]
❏ Excessive valve clearances [3]

G. High-pitched whir

Sounds like: Very high-speed zing that rapidly increases in frequency.

CAUSES:

❏ Starter still energized or engaged [3]

VIBRATION

A. Low-frequency vibration

Components moving and turning at slower speeds.

CAUSES:

❏ Natural resonance—see note at right [1]
❏ Damaged or dirty propeller [2]
❏ Engine misfiring [3]
❏ Propeller-shaft coupling loose [3]
❏ Bent prop shaft [4]
❏ Flywheel loose [5]

B. Medium-frequency vibration

The majority of vibration at a frequency close to engine rpm.

CAUSES:

❏ Engine mounts loose [2]
❏ Engine misfiring [3]
❏ Flywheel loose [5]

C. High-frequency vibration

Components moving and turning at very high speeds.

CAUSES:

❏ Starter stuck/engaged [3]
❏ Alternator fan out of balance [3]

Note: Smaller engines with 1, 2, or 3 cylinders will often vibrate violently at slower rpm. This is particularly noticeable with lighter, alloy engines whose softer mounts are optimized for the smoothest running at operating rpm. All engines have rpm bands where the vibration is greater. Often the vibration is more pronounced because of poor installation.

CHART
8

STARTING SYSTEM PROBLEMS

Problems with the starting system account for a high percentage of diesel engine faults. Diesel engines ignite fuel by compressing air in the cylinders to generate heat. The speed at which a starter turns over the engine has a major effect on cylinder pressures. Keeping the starting system in top condition is even more important in cold weather, when much of the heat is robbed by cold cylinders and cylinder heads, batteries produce less power, and thicker oil creates increased drag.

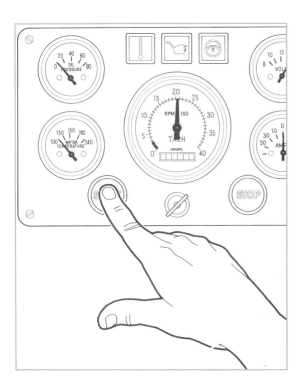

NOTHING HAPPENS WHEN THE IGNITION IS SWITCHED ON

No indication of power to the instrument panel. Water temperature and oil pressure gauges fail to "zero," no warning lights, and no buzzer.

CAUSES:

❑ Battery selector switched off [1]
❑ Battery-ground isolation switch off [1]
❑ Battery voltage very low [1]
❑ Loose or broken wiring [2]
❑ Defective ignition switch [2]

NO RESPONSE WHEN STARTER IS SELECTED

Water temperature and oil pressure gauges "zero," panel lights and buzzers work, but there is no response from the starter when selected.

CAUSES:

❑ Battery voltage low [1]
❑ Loose or corroded connections [2]
❑ Defective ignition/start switch [3]
❑ Poor ground connection on engine [3]
❑ Broken wiring [3]

STARTER TURNS SLOWLY OR JUST "CLICKS"

Power is evident at the instrument panel. Selecting "start" causes the starter to turn the engine over very slowly or the solenoid to energize and just "click."

A. Solenoid "clicks" once—battery voltage drops

The click indicates power has energized the starter solenoid. A voltage drop indicated by the voltmeter or dimming lights shows the starter is drawing high amperage.

CAUSES:

- ❏ Engine seized [3]
- ❏ Starter shorting internally [3]
- ❏ Starter jammed in flywheel ring gear [4]
- ❏ Starter seized [4]

B. Solenoid "clicks" once—battery voltage remains high

Power has energized the starter solenoid but is not getting to the starter motor.

CAUSES:

- ❏ Starter solenoid not making contact [2]
- ❏ Starter positive supply not connected or loose [3]
- ❏ Engine ground wire not connected or loose [3]

C. Solenoid "clicks" repeatedly

Power has energized the solenoid, but the voltage drop is so great when the starter is energized that the solenoid disengages. Voltage recovers and the solenoid energizes, and the cycle repeats, creating a rapid clicking sound.

CAUSES:

- ❏ Battery voltage low [1]
- ❏ Loose or corroded connections [2]

STARTER OVERSPEEDS OR REMAINS ENGAGED

When the starter is selected, the engine fails to turn over and is accompanied by a high-pitched whirring.

A. Starter overspeed occurs when "start" is selected

The starter is getting power, but the spinning gear is not engaging with the flywheel ring gear.

CAUSES:

- ❏ Clutch slipping [2]
- ❏ Dirt, wear, or corrosion on starter shaft preventing the gear from engaging [3]
- ❏ Bendix-type starter—Bendix defective [3]

B. Starter overspeed continues when not selected

The solenoid is jammed in the energized position with the starter gear not engaging.

CAUSES:

- ❏ Defective solenoid [2]
- ❏ Defective start switch [3]

Warning: This problem can be serious. You can only stop the starter from turning by disconnecting the power. If your starting system is well designed, the engine battery switch will kill power. Some systems have a ground-isolation switch that will have the same effect. If you have neither, the starter will spin until it has drained all the battery power. More likely, it will burn out the wiring or the starter will overheat and the commutator explode. Make sure your wiring is correct before this occurs and burns your boat to the waterline!

C. Starter continues engaged after the switch is deselected—see warning above

CAUSES:

- ❏ Defective solenoid [2]
- ❏ Defective start switch [3]
- ❏ Damaged starter gear or flywheel ring gear [4]

CHART
9

CHARGING SYSTEM PROBLEMS

As their name suggests, alternators produce alternating current which is rectified into the direct current that powers the boat's electrical equipment. Output is controlled by a voltage regulator, which senses battery voltage and varies the current fed to the rotor windings. Higher current increases rotor magnetism, which induces higher output from the stator windings. All alternators work on the same principle, although output will vary with size and regulator design.

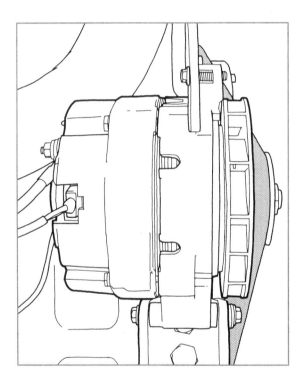

NO CHARGING

Indications of alternator not charging are:
- Ignition warning light fails to extinguish.
- No voltage increase at the alternator output terminal.
- No voltage increase at the battery terminal.
- Alternator does not get warm/hot.
- No indication on the ammeter.

CAUSES:

❑ V-belt slipping or broken	[1]
❑ Output wire disconnected, broken, loose, or corroded	[2]
❑ Ground connection poor	[2]
❑ Regulator failed—open circuit	[2]
❑ Stator or rotor coils defective	[3]
❑ Rectifier defective	[3]
❑ Brushes worn or broken	[3]

HOW LIKELY?   [1] Very common   [2] Common   [3] Possible   [4] Rare   [5] Very rare

UNDERCHARGING

Indications of undercharging are:
- Minimal voltage increase on the engine panel voltmeter.
- Batteries fail to fully charge.

CAUSES:
- ❏ Insufficient charge time   [1]
- ❏ V-belt slipping   [1]
- ❏ Output connection loose or corroded   [2]
- ❏ Ground connection loose or corroded   [2]
- ❏ Brushes worn   [3]
- ❏ Slip rings contaminated or worn   [3]
- ❏ Stator or rotor coils defective   [3]
- ❏ Rectifier defective   [3]

OVERCHARGING

Indications of overcharging are:
- Battery very hot.
- Electrolyte boiling violently.
- Strong acid smell.
- Voltmeter reading over 14.5 volts.
- Low electrolyte level.

CAUSES:
- ❏ Battery-voltage sensing wire broken, loose, corroded, or disconnected   [2]
- ❏ Regulator failed—short circuit   [2]
- ❏ Battery defective   [2]

CHART
10

TURBOCHARGER PROBLEMS

These faults are applicable only to engines fitted with turbochargers and are in addition to faults covered in the other charts.

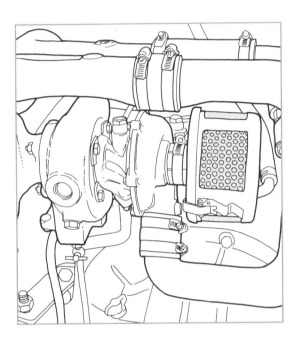

NOISE

A. Hissing air

The increased air pressure created by the turbocharger compressor is usually less than the 20 psi when the engine is running at maximum rpm. It is unlikely that escaping air can be heard over the noise of the engine and turbocharger.

CAUSES:

❏ Gaskets leaking between compressor
outlet and inlet manifold   [3]

B. Surging

Surging is the breakdown of airflow over the compressor blades during rapid acceleration. The result is a series of pressure surges as the intake air momentarily reverses direction. The noise created is difficult to describe but sounds like very fast popping or rasping.

CAUSES:

❏ Dirty turbocharger   [2]
❏ Turbocharger binding   [3]

EXCESSIVE SMOKE

A. Black/dark smoke
Dark smoke indicates partially burned fuel, usually caused by excessive fuel or a reduced air supply.

CAUSES:

- ❏ Restricted air filter [2]
- ❏ Compressor dirty [2]
- ❏ Intercooler dirty [2]
- ❏ Air leak from intake pipes downstream of compressor [3]
- ❏ Turbocharger binding [3]
- ❏ Restricted exhaust-gas flow [3]
- ❏ Exhaust-gas leak before turbocharger [3]
- ❏ Turbocharger seized [4]

B. Blue smoke
White exhaust smoke with a hint of blue indicates burned oil.

CAUSES:

- ❏ Turbocharger shaft seals leaking [2]
- ❏ Turbocharger oil-return pipe clogged [4]

PERFORMANCE PROBLEMS

Turbocharged engines produce more power for their size because the greater quantity of air in the cylinders allows more fuel to be burned. Any reduction in turbocharger efficiency can have a marked effect on performance.

CAUSES:

- ❏ Restricted air filter [2]
- ❏ Turbocharger dirty [2]
- ❏ Intercooler dirty [2]

- ❏ Turbocharger binding [3]
- ❏ Air leak from intake pipes downstream of turbocharger [3]
- ❏ Restricted exhaust-gas flow [3]
- ❏ Turbocharger seized [4]
- ❏ Exhaust-gas leak before turbocharger [4]

VIBRATION

A. Very high frequency
Turbochargers rotate at very high speeds—often close to 200,000 rpm. At this speed, the smallest of uneven forces will cause high-frequency vibrations that can be destructive.

CAUSES:

- ❏ Turbine/shaft/compressor assembly out of balance. Possible broken or damaged blades [3]
- ❏ Excessive bearing wear [3]
- ❏ Compressor or turbine making contact with casing [3]

B. Low frequency

CAUSES:

- ❏ Loose pipes and fittings [4]

CHART
11

FUEL SYSTEM FUNCTIONAL CHECK

The following procedure can be carried out by anyone with a few basic tools. If your engine will not start, is difficult to start, or dies soon after starting, this check will confirm whether the fuel system is the cause. It will also identify many other problems that can cause low power, rough running, and excessive smoke.

START

Is the fuel turned off?
Is the stop cable pulled out? (very common)
Have you turned off any fuel supply or return valves?
Is the fuel tank empty?
Could there be air in the fuel?
Is starting difficult after carrying out maintenance on fuel system?

Yes →

Bleed the fuel system of air
The injector pump will not work with air in the fuel system. Although some pumps can self-bleed, all air should be removed from the system any time it is disturbed.
While operating the manual lever on the lift pump, bleed air from:
1. The bleed screw on the secondary filter.
2. All bleed screws on the injector pump.

No ↓

Confirm fuel is reaching the injectors
The quickest method of checking the fuel system is to confirm fuel is reaching the injectors. Loosen all the injector supply lines at the injector. Turn the engine over using the starter.
Does a small shot of fuel spurt from each injector line?

Yes →

The injector pump is suspect
The injector pump is not delivering high pressure fuel to the injectors, despite having a good supply of air-free fuel. If you have just serviced part of the fuel system, the most likely cause is air in the injector pump. Follow your service manual's instructions carefully on bleeding air out of the pump. If the pump still fails to deliver a shot of fuel at the injector-inlet connection, it is probable your injector pump is defective. Pump failure is not very common, so consider bleeding the system again before replacing a very expensive component.
Injector pumps can only be rebuilt by diesel shops that have the specialized test equipment. If defective, replace it with a new or reconditioned unit.

No ↓

Check the low-pressure fuel system
Unscrew the bleed screw from the secondary fuel filter. Turn the engine over using the starter.
Does airless fuel flow full-bore in spurts?

Yes →

No ↓

Check the lift pump and secondary filter
Disconnect the fuel supply line to the lift pump, and replace it with a hose with one end dipped in a container of clean fuel. Turn the engine over on the starter once more.
Does airless fuel flow full-bore in spurts?

Yes →

The fuel supply to the engine is suspect
Fuel is not reaching the lift pump. The most common cause is a restricted element or poor sealing on the primary filter, which is letting air into the system. If the filter checks out okay then inspect the fuel hoses and connections. The fuel tank pickup tube or vent could be blocked.

No ↓

Check the lift pump
With the fuel supply still from a separate container, disconnect the fuel-outlet line from the lift pump. Turn the engine over on the starter once more.
Does airless fuel flow full-bore in spurts?

Yes →

The secondary fuel filter is suspect
Check that the secondary filter is not clogged and that hoses, pipes, and connections are good. A poor connection after the lift pump sees low pressure fuel and will leak fuel rather than suck in air.

No ↓

The lift pump is suspect
Before condemning the lift pump, remove it from the engine and operate the actuator lever. The pump should make rude noises as the diaphragm sucks in air and expels it past small non-return valves. A finger over the inlet and outlet should feel good suction and pressure, respectively. Some engines have an additional external valve on the pump inlet that is prone to sticking shut.

Confirm the injectors are good
Remove all the injectors from the cylinder head. Then refit each injector back into its fuel line so you can see the nozzle. Leave return lines disconnected during this procedure. Turn engine over using the starter and note the spray pattern from each injector nozzle.
Warning: High-pressure fuel can penetrate skin and cause infection. Be sure to keep clear of the spray.
Do all the injectors produce a finely atomized spray with no dripping from the nozzle?

The injectors are suspect
Defective injectors must be replaced. Although an engine will run with worn or contaminated injectors, starting will become progressively more difficult with an accompanying increase of smoke from the exhaust. If a telltale rainbow slick of fuel is visible on the water surface by the exhaust, it's a sure sign that the injectors need servicing.
Although some service manuals show how injectors can be disassembled for cleaning, this task requires special test equipment to ensure injectors are "popping" at the correct pressure and are producing the correct pattern of finely atomized fuel.

Check that the cold-starting device is being used correctly
Some engines do not need the cold-starting device for starting in warm climates. Most diesels will not start without one in colder climates.
Warning: Never use ether starting aids with heater-type cold-starting devices. The consequences can be explosive!
Is the cold-starting device being used for the recommended time?

Use the correct starting procedure
Usually preheat devices are operated for 30 seconds before the starter is engaged. If you are not sure of the correct procedure, check the operator's manual.

Check that the cold-starting device is working
Cold-starting devices vary among manufacturers. Confirm which type is fitted and then check that it is operating correctly.
Is the cold-starting device working?

Cold-starting device is suspect
Nearly all cold-starting devices use a sealed heating element that cannot be repaired and must be replaced if suspect.

The return line may be restricted
Depending on the engine, return lines carry surplus and aerated fuel back to the top of the fuel tank. On some injector pumps, a blocked or restricted return line will affect its performance. Although you may not have a problem if no fuel appears from the return line, it is a good idea to disconnect both ends to confirm there is no restriction.

Check the injector return line is not restricted
Disconnect the return line close to the fuel tank. Place the line into a bucket and try running the engine.
Does fuel flow into the bucket?

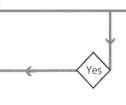

Fuel system appears to be functioning correctly
The checks you have carried out suggest there is no problem with the fuel system. You should have checked the following:
❑ Fuel is reaching the injectors.
❑ All the injectors are producing finely atomized fuel in a good spray pattern.
❑ The cold-starting device is working.
❑ The return line is not blocked.
There are several other reasons why the fuel system may not still be performing correctly, but they are less common and should be tackled only by an experienced mechanic.

CHART

12

ENGINE FAILS TO STOP

Before you press the start button, you should know how to shut down the engine. It's also advisable to know what type of shutdown mechanism is fitted and how to stop the engine if it fails.

EMERGENCY SHUTDOWN

If the engine fails to stop, identify the type of shutdown mechanism and check out the following methods first.

A. Cable/mechanical shutdown

1. Locate the engine end of the cable.
2. Operate the shutdown lever by hand.

B. Electrical solenoid "energized to run"

1. Locate the solenoid, which usually is fitted to the injector pump.
2. Disconnect the power-supply cable.

C. Electrical solenoid "energized to stop"

1. Locate the solenoid.
2. If shutdown lever is remotely mounted, operate by hand.
3. Otherwise, if solenoid is fitted to injector pump, use a lead to jump power from the positive supply on the starter or battery to the solenoid.

D. If all else fails

1. Stop the intake airflow by blocking the air intake. Be very careful not to let anything get sucked into the intake!
   OR
2. Loosen the injector supply lines.
   OR
3. Shut off the fuel supply. Remember: You will have to bleed the fuel system before the engine will start again.

MECHANICAL STOP LEVER

A push-pull cable operates a shutdown lever fitted to the injector pump or governor. Failures are mostly cable problems that can be overridden by operating the pump shutdown lever by hand.

CAUSES:

❏ Cable disconnected at engine   [2]
❏ Cable broken or seized   [3]
❏ Governor lever seized or binding   [3]

HOW LIKELY?   [1] Very common   [2] Common   [3] Possible   [4] Rare   [5] Very rare

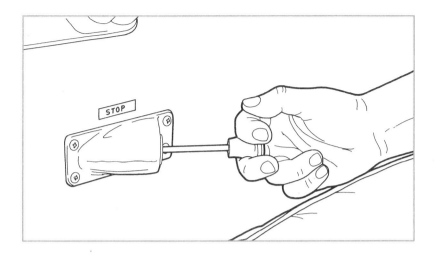

ELECTRICAL STOP BUTTON

Electrical shutdowns differ with engine design. The main types are:

- ❏ External solenoid that pulls a fuel shutoff lever on the injector pump or governor
- ❏ Integral solenoid fitted to the injector pump that controls the pump's fuel supply
- ❏ Integral solenoid fitted to in-line injector pumps that pulls the fuel rack to a shutoff position

A. "Energized to run" type

The solenoid is permanently energized while the engine runs. Power is cut off to stop the engine. Disconnecting the lead at the solenoid should shut down the engine. This method is mainly used on generators.

CAUSES:

❏ Solenoid sticking	[3]
❏ Injector-pump fuel rack sticking	[3]
❏ Shut down relay defective	[3]

B. "Energized to stop" type

This type of solenoid is energized only when the stop button is pressed. If the engine fails to stop, voltage is probably not reaching the solenoid. If it has an external solenoid, try operating the lever manually.

CAUSES:

❏ Voltage not reading solenoid	[1]
❏ Solenoid mechanical linkage disconnected	[2]
❏ Solenoid or linkage sticking	[3]
❏ Injector-pump fuel rack sticking	[3]
❏ Solenoid travel incorrectly set	[3]

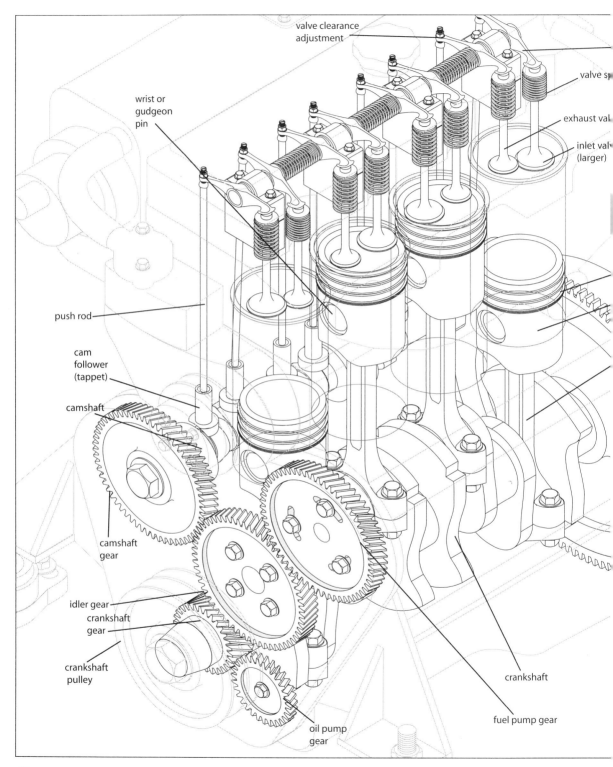

valve clearance
adjustment

valve s

exhaust val

inlet val
(larger)

wrist or
gudgeon
pin

push rod

cam
follower
(tappet)

camshaft

camshaft
gear

idler gear

crankshaft
gear

crankshaft
pulley

oil pump
gear

crankshaft

fuel pump gear

rocker arm

piston ring

piston

connecting
rod

flywheel

flywheel
ring gear

3

THE
MECHANICAL SYSTEM

The engine block, cylinder head, and a host of reciprocating and rotating components harness the force of the exploding diesel/air mixture and transmit combustion energy through the flywheel to the transmission. These components are extremely reliable, requiring no routine maintenance other than the occasional valve-clearance adjustment.

Mechanical problems can often be traced to failures in other systems—particularly the lubrication and exhaust systems—which can cause severe damage to bearing surfaces. Rectification often entails major work, but you can make many of these repairs yourself, without purchasing special tools or removing the engine. Even an experienced mechanic, however, will need a repair or shop manual that details the correct strip, inspection, and assembly procedures.

ENGINE BLOCK

The cylinder block of a diesel engine is machined from a complex casting that includes locations for the cylinder liners, crankshaft, camshaft, engine mounts, oil galleries, and waterways; it is designed to take the high loads and thermal stresses imposed by the moving components. The block requires no routine maintenance.

FREEZE PLUGS

Freeze plugs protect block and head castings in the event that the coolant freezes. They will normally last the life of an engine if the cooling system is well maintained. If not, these steel plugs will corrode; check them regularly. The

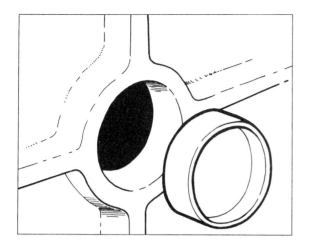

first sign of a problem will appear as a pinhole slowly weeping coolant. If one plug fails, replace all the freeze plugs.

CYLINDER HEAD

The cylinder head must fit tightly onto the engine block to maintain a good seal at the top of each cylinder. Uneven tightness leads to air, oil, and coolant leaks and may induce high stresses that can warp and crack the cylinder head. Most engines require the cylinder head bolts be retorqued after the first 50 hours of running to compensate for settling of the cylinder head gasket.

CYLINDER-HEAD GASKET

The first sign of head-gasket trouble is often a slight bubbling or fluid leak at the joint between the engine block and the cylinder head. More serious leakage can cause difficult starting, rough running, and loss of power. With severe leakage, the coolant pressure cap will vent coolant as combustion gases escape across the gasket into the coolant circuit.

Although retorquing the cylinder-head bolts will often stop small leaks, it's better to remove the cylinder head and replace the gasket. Leave this task to the more experienced with access to a

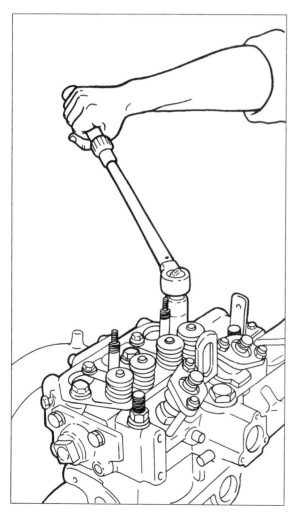

shop manual and torque wrench. Don't forget: Retorque the new gasket after 50 hours of operation.

CRANKSHAFT

The largest moving component in the engine, the crankshaft converts the reciprocating movement of the pistons into the rotary movement that drives the propeller shaft. Crankshafts are forged from high-quality steel to withstand high stresses.

The crankshaft requires no routine maintenance and will run for thousands of hours with minimal wear if you change the lubricating oil regularly.

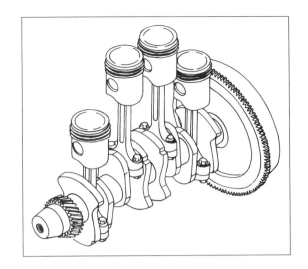

TIMING GEARS

Timing gears rotate the camshaft at half crankshaft speed and ensure that the inlet and exhaust valves open and close at the correct point in the four-stroke cycle. They also drive the high-pressure fuel pump. The engine manufacturer sets the timing at assembly by aligning the gears that connect the camshaft to the crankshaft. Unless the engine has been stripped and incorrectly reassembled, the timing will not change and needs no adjustment.

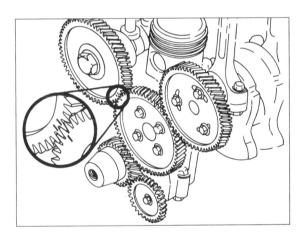

VALVES

Small clearances between the valve stems and rocker arms compensate for thermal expansion. These valve clearances change with normal wear and need occasional adjustment.

The engine shop manual—and sometimes the owner's manual—will list the correct clearance, which often differs between the inlet and exhaust valves. Adjustment is straightforward, unless the engine has an overhead camshaft in the cylinder head and uses special shims to alter clearances.

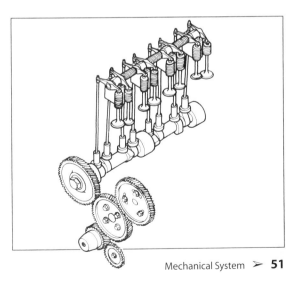

CHECKING AND ADJUSTING VALVE CLEARANCES

Adjust valve clearances with the engine cold and the valve fully closed, with its cam follower off the camshaft lobe. Placing the piston on or near top dead center (TDC) on the compression stroke ensures that both the inlet and exhaust valves are fully closed.

1. Place the #1 cylinder—usually the one nearest the front of the engine— at TDC on the compression stroke. On an engine with TDC alignment marks on the crankshaft pulley or flywheel, turn it slowly clockwise (as viewed from the front) until the marks align *just* after the intake valve for the #1 cylinder closes. On an engine with no alignment marks, turn it slowly until the #1-cylinder intake valve closes fully, then turn another 90°; this will place the camshaft in a good position.

2. Measure the gap, or clearance, of the intake and exhaust valves with a feeler gauge. The gauge should just slip between the top of the valve stem and the rocker arm.

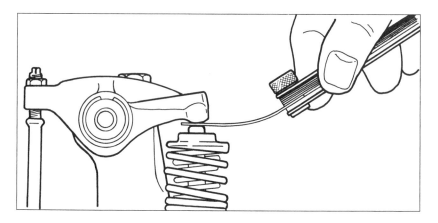

3. Adjusting the clearance almost requires three hands to hold the feeler gauge and adjustment screw while locking the nut. Always recheck the clearance after locking the nut.
4. Repeat for all cylinders. Continue rotating the crankshaft clockwise until the intake valve of the next cylinder fully closes; turn another 90° and then check that cylinder's valve clearance.

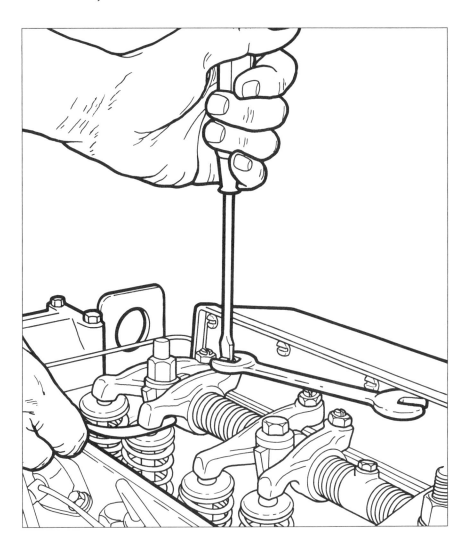

PISTONS AND CYLINDERS

Pistons and cylinders work extremely hard and therefore wear more than any other engine component. Fortunately, the process is gradual, and with frequent oil changes, a good intake-air filter, and well-maintained injectors, they will give thousands of hours of service before demanding attention.

Difficult starting, loss of power, and excessive smoking are typical symptoms of severe cylinder wear. But these symptoms might also signify that one cylinder's rings are stuck in the piston grooves, or perhaps that one of the inlet or exhaust valves is not seating well. Before condemning an engine or stripping it for a major overhaul, test its compression.

TESTING COMPRESSION

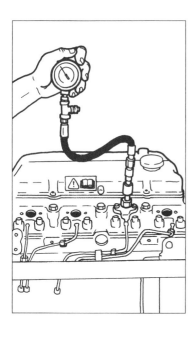

The compression tester consists of a dummy injector connected to a 0–600–psi gauge. A small non-return valve retains the maximum pressure. All the injectors are removed and each cylinder tested, using the starter motor to turn over the engine. Initially, the test is carried out "dry"; then a small amount of oil is added to each cylinder and the test repeated.

A comparison between cylinders will identify those with lower pressures. If the suspect cylinder increases pressure dramatically when tested "wet," the problem lies with worn piston rings and cylinders. No change when wet suggests leaking valve seats.

It sounds simple in theory, but in practice the volume of the dummy injector, hose, and gauge affects the indicated pressure, as do the state of the battery, condition of the starter, viscosity of the oil, and temperature. Compression should be carried out by a professional who has a good "feel" for the pressures an engine will produce with his or her test equipment. Compression testing tends to be comparative but is really effective in identifying problems in individual cylinders.

MAJOR OVERHAUL

Excessive wear on the piston rings and cylinder bores can mean costly repairs. Weigh carefully the many hours of labor to repair an older engine versus the cost of fitting a new one—especially if you lack the skills and are considering hiring a professional mechanic. Information on overhaul procedure is detailed in the manufacturer's repair or shop manual.

ENGINE MOUNTS

Most installations use flexible engine mounts to help absorb vibration. In ideal conditions, these mounts require no maintenance. Unfortunately, conditions are far from ideal below a leaky engine, close to the bilge.

INSPECTION

Check that all adjustment nuts are tight. Lower nuts tend to wind down. Black or rusty dust indicates loose mounts that are fretting. Check that the bolts holding the mounts to the engine bed are tight. Rubber should not be split or separating from the metal. Corroded mounts make engine alignment impossible and should be replaced. Treat all mounts regularly with a heavy-duty corrosion inhibitor.

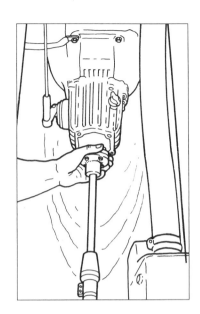

ENGINE ALIGNMENT

An engine out of alignment with its propeller shaft will cause excessive bearing friction, which can increase stern-gear noise and considerably reduce power. A large alignment error will bend the prop shaft on each revolution. Couplings will work loose, transmission bearings and seals will fail, and eventually the prop shaft itself will fatigue and break.

QUICK-AND-EASY CHECK

If you can turn the shaft by hand without feeling any tight spots, the alignment is probably close.

MEASURING AND CORRECTING ALIGNMENT ERRORS

Measuring alignment along the three major axes is straightforward, but correcting errors is not. Each adjustment on one axis affects the other two. Engine alignment is not complicated, but it may take several hours and try your patience.

Remove the coupling bolts; then turn the shaft several times to *just* separate the two halves of the coupling. If the length of prop shaft between the coupling and stern gland is substantial, support the shaft to keep it in position. If a flexible coupling is used, alignment procedures vary with coupling manufacturer. If in doubt, remove it.

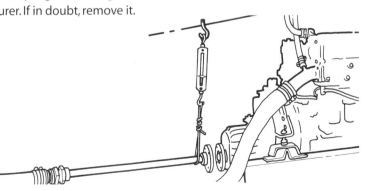

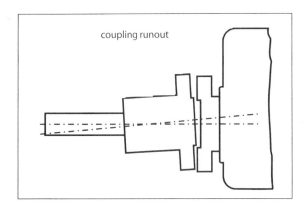

coupling runout

1. COUPLING RUNOUT

To determine the *coupling runout error,* measure the gap between the faces at the top and bottom with feeler gauges and subtract the smaller number to get the vertical error. (For example, 0.024 inches at the top and 0.013 inches at the bottom show a gap of 0.024 – 0.013 = 0.011 inches at the top.) Now, rotate only the shaft half of the coupling 90° and recheck. If the gap changes dramatically, the shaft coupling is incorrectly machined or fitted, or the shaft itself is bent.

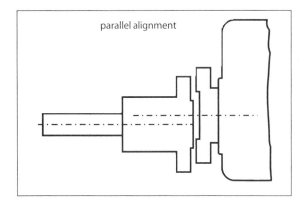

parallel alignment

2. PARALLEL ALIGNMENT

Measure *parallel alignment* by bringing the two halves of the coupling together and placing a straightedge across the top. Measure any gap beneath the straightedge with feeler gauges. Repeat at the bottom and sides of the couplings. Maximum permitted error is 0.005 inches for small couplings; correct any greater error by adjusting all the engine mounts evenly in the same direction.

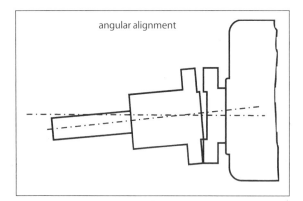

angular alignment

3. ANGULAR ALIGNMENT

For *angular alignment,* measure the top and bottom gap between the coupling faces and subtract the smaller number to get the vertical error. The maximum permitted error is 0.001 inches for each 1 inch of coupling diameter. In other words, a coupling measuring 5 inches diameter should have a gap of 0.005 inches or less. To close a gap at the top of the coupling, either raise the front mounts or lower the rear mounts. For a gap at the bottom, do the opposite. Repeat the measurement side to side to get the horizontal error. To close a gap on the port side, slide the aft mounts to starboard or the front mounts to port. For a gap on the starboard side, do the opposite.

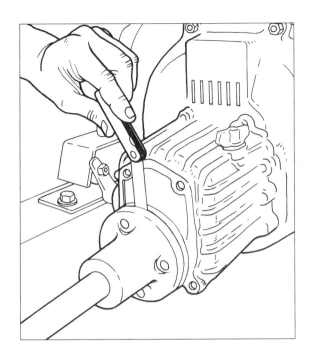

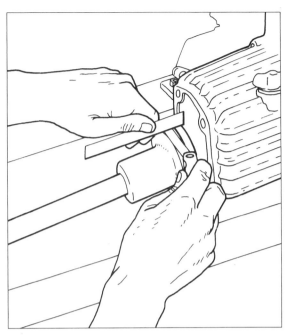

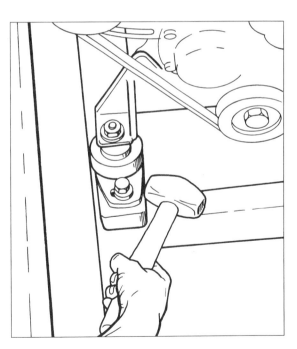

MECHANICAL SYSTEM FAULTS

Problem	Possible Cause	Possible Symptoms

CRANKSHAFT ASSEMBLY

Problem	Possible Cause	Possible Symptoms
Crankshaft broken	Fatigue [5]	Engine will not run and makes unusual noise
Flywheel loose	Poor assembly [4] Broken locking device [5]	Severe vibration; knocking
Connecting rod bent or broken	Water in cylinder [2] Broken valve [3] Incorrect timing [4]	Erratic rpm; loss of power; difficult starting; compression low
Rod bearing loose	Poor assembly [4] Broken bolt [4]	Hard mechanical knocking
Rod bearings worn	Excessive wear [3] Poor lubrication [3]	As above
Front pulley loose	Poor assembly [4] Broken locking device [5]	V-belt thrown; vibration

PISTONS AND CYLINDERS

Problem	Possible Cause	Possible Symptoms
Piston seized	Corrosion [2] Overheating [3] Poor lubrication [4]	Engine seized; water in cylinders
Piston knocking	Piston rings picking up on bore [4] Broken valve [4] Rod bearings worn [4] Incorrect valve timing [5]	Loud knocking, particularly at high rpm
Piston rings worn	Tired engine [3]	Poor compression; loss of power; high oil consumption; difficult starting; blue exhaust smoke
Cylinder liner cracked	Overheating [4] Corrosion [5]	Coolant in oil; coolant in cylinder
Cylinder liner scored	Poor intake-air filtration [2] Poor lubrication [3]	High oil consumption; blue exhaust smoke

CYLINDER HEAD

Problem	Possible Cause	Possible Symptoms
Cracked	Overheating [3] Adding cold water to overheated engine [3] Incorrect torque on bolts [4]	Coolant in oil; oil in coolant; loss of power; difficult starting
Warped	Incorrect torque on head bolts [2] Overheating [3]	Leaking cylinder-head gasket—see below
Gasket leaking	Incorrect torque on head bolts [2] Warped head [4]	Coolant in oil; oil in coolant; loss of power; difficult starting; water in cylinders; slight bubbling from joint

VALVE GEAR

Problem	Possible Cause	Possible Symptoms
Valve stuck open	Valve stem contaminated with carbon [3] Corrosion [3] Valve bent [3] Poor lubrication [4]	Loss of compression; uneven running; poor starting; excessive exhaust smoke
Valve seat leaking	Seat damaged, eroded, or worn [2] Valve bent [3] Inadequate valve clearance [4]	Loss of compression; fuel mixture forced out of inlet manifold (inlet valve); excessive exhaust smoke
Valve guides worn	Tired engine [3]	High oil consumption; blue exhaust smoke
Valve spring broken	Fatigue—usually from operation at very high rpm [3]	Knocking; loss of power; difficult starting; excessive exhaust smoke
Excessive valve clearance	Normal wear on valve gear [1] Incorrect adjustment [2]	Rattling sound from the valve cover; slight loss in performance
Reduced valve clearance	Incorrect adjustment [2] Valve seat or face worn [3]	Loss of performance
Camshaft broken	Fatigue [5]	Engine fails to run; pistons hitting valves; engine running rough
Push rod bent	Incorrect valve clearances [3] Seized valve [3] Incorrect timing [5]	Loss of performance

ENGINE MOUNTS

Problem	Possible Cause	Possible Symptoms
Loose, broken, delaminated	Vibration [2] Poor assembly [2] Oil contamination [3]	Vibration; loss of power; prop shaft difficult to turn

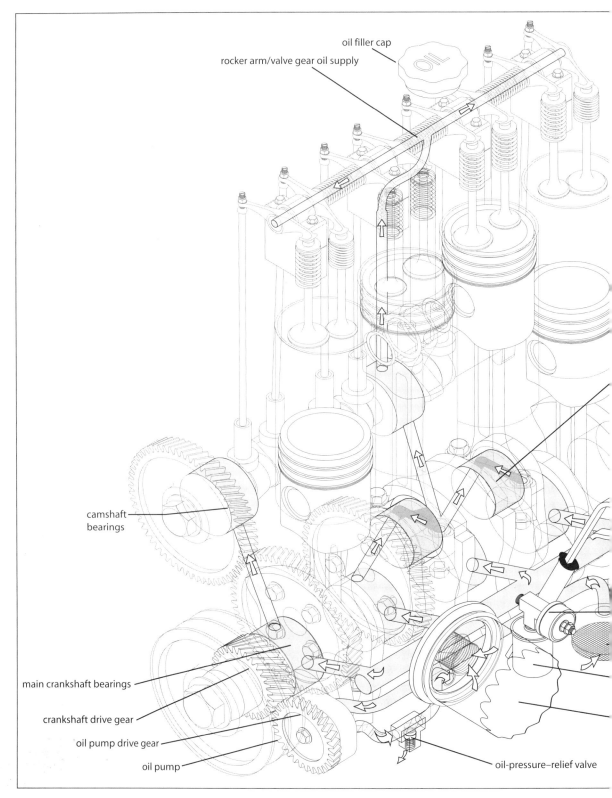

oil filler cap

rocker arm/valve gear oil supply

camshaft bearings

main crankshaft bearings

crankshaft drive gear

oil pump drive gear

oil pump

oil-pressure–relief valve

4
THE
LUBRICATION SYSTEM

connecting
rod
bearings

main oil
gallery

dipstick

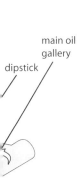

low–oil-pressure
warning switch

oil strainer

oil-pressure–gauge
sender

oil filter

To minimize friction and wear, a diesel engine's complex lubrication system maintains a thin film of oil on the contact surfaces of hundreds of moving metal parts. The oil system also plays an important role in removing excess heat from pistons and cylinder walls. Without oil, the heat of metal-to-metal contact would melt bearings and piston rings within seconds.

Maintaining the oil system is straightforward: Use a good-quality oil of the appropriate grade; monitor levels; and keep it clean by changing both oil and filter frequently. With normal use, oil loses its lubricating and cleaning properties as the level of contaminants rises. Replace the oil before it reaches that point.

Common lubrication system problems include minor leaks, which are usually just cosmetically objectionable; and oil contamination, which requires immediate action.

OIL

The quality of your oil and the frequency with which you change it are major determinants of your engine's life.

CHECKING THE LEVEL

Check the oil level before you start the engine. If you must check it after the engine has run, give the oil time to settle into the pan before pulling the dipstick. Wipe any splashed oil off the dipstick and reinsert it fully to get a reading. The level should be close to the high mark. Never run the engine if the oil level is outside the dipstick marks. Too little oil, and you risk seizing the

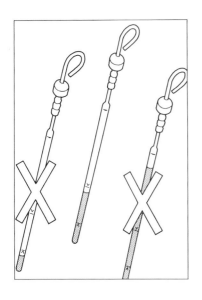

engine; too much, and the crankshaft will dip into the oil, causing aeration, overheating, and uncontrollable over-revvings. Black oil is normal for a diesel, but watch for sludge, milkiness, a thin quality, diesel smell, or particles in the oil.

WHICH GRADE?

Oil should meet the American Petroleum Industry (API) CF-4 or CG-4 requirements. These "C" grades indicate that the oil is designed for diesel engines. (Gasoline engines use "S" grade oils.) Many good oils will work in both diesel and gas engines, but always check both engine and oil specifications first.

WHICH VISCOSITY?

Stick with the engine manufacturer's recommendations. Temperature affects viscosity dramatically: A low ambient temperature calls for thin oil; a high ambient temperature calls for thick. Too thin, and lubrication qualities suffer; too thick, and components will drag, starting will be difficult, and again, lubricating properties will be poor.

Multigrade oils have proven more effective than single-grade oils at reducing engine wear, especially during cold startup; their lower viscosity creates less drag and allows oil to reach bearing surfaces more rapidly. Reduced deposits on the piston rings allow the rings to move more easily, with consequent better sealing. This results in less oil in the combustion chamber—reducing oil consumption and smoke.

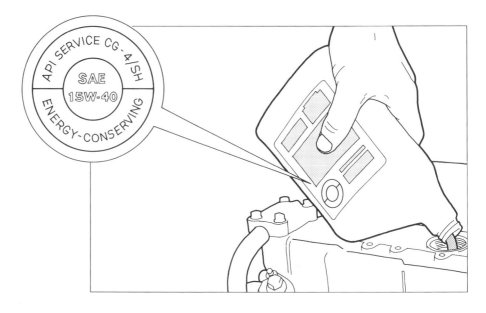

SAE VISCOSITY GRADES

Ambient Temperature

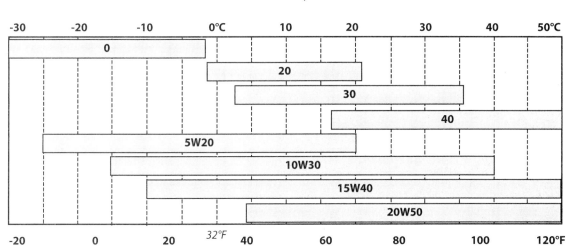

Ambient Temperature

OIL ADDITIVES

Oil manufacturers use additives to improve the properties and extend the life of an oil. Today's oils combat soot, sludge, and varnish buildup, neutralize acids, and fight condensation—all while maintaining good viscosity. Antiwear and antiscuff additives extend engine life. After-market additives, however, have limited effect, and are not really cost effective. You'd do better to change the oil and filter more frequently.

OIL LEAKS

Nearly all engines leak oil to some extent from seals and openings. Early designs placed less emphasis on gaskets and seals, so expect more leakage in older engines. External leaks become more pronounced with age and use and can be a good indication of engine life and its quality of maintenance.

OIL CONSUMPTION

All diesels burn oil to some extent, but usually in such small quantities as to be barely noticeable between oil changes. Other than the blue smoke it produces, oil consumption is not a problem and alone is seldom cause for rebuilding an engine.

OIL PRESSURE

Many factors affect oil pressure, especially oil grade, age, and temperature. As bearings wear and clearances increase, the oil system must work harder to maintain pressure. Oil pressure can therefore be a very good indicator of engine condition. Pressures are typically 40–60 psi at idle on cold startup and must show within 15 seconds (if not, shut down the engine).

At high rpm, these pressures should be maintained but will drop as temperatures increase. When returned to idle, a hot engine may show pressures below 20 psi.

Low pressure throughout the rpm range may indicate a well-used engine, but check the specifications—some low-pressure/high-flow systems are rated as low as 8 psi!

CHANGING OIL

With automotive-engine manufacturers continually stretching the time between servicing, it becomes tempting to squeeze in an extra few hours between oil changes on your boat's diesel. Don't! Changing the oil often will prolong that expensive diesel's life. Follow the manufacturer's recommended oil-change frequencies *as a minimum*. In general, change oil every 125 hours or seasonally, whichever comes first.

If your fuel has a high sulfur content, you need a heavy-duty oil to handle the sulfur. Alternatively, double the frequency of oil changes.

DRAINING OIL

A little forethought can make the messy job of changing oil much easier—and the easier it is, the less likely you'll be to put it off. Place oil-absorbent pads beneath the filter and drain plug to catch wayward spills before they reach the bilge. Run the engine just before changing the oil to get all the contaminants off the bottom of the pan and suspended in the oil. Warm oil will drain more quickly than cold oil. With a good-sized container close by, remove the drain plug at the bottom of the pan. Inevitably, the plug will slip from your fingers and fall into the container, just as the warm oil gushes everywhere *except* the container. No wonder changing the oil is one of the most hated routine-maintenance tasks.

If you use an oil pump to suck oil out through the dipstick tube, be sure the pickup tube reaches the bottom of the sump. Many marine diesels have a manual oil pump connected to the pan drain plug, which makes oil changes much easier and cleaner.

If your engine has no pump, consider installing one. Simply replace the drain plug with a threaded hose barb. (Take care to match the threads of the barb to the pan; some manufacturers use threads other than the standard NPT.) Fix the pump in an accessible location, connect the barb and pump with an oil-resistant hose, and clamp them securely. Do not use the popular clear polyester braided hose; it will harden and crack within a season.

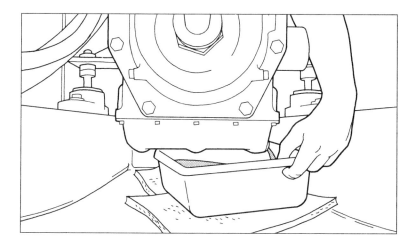

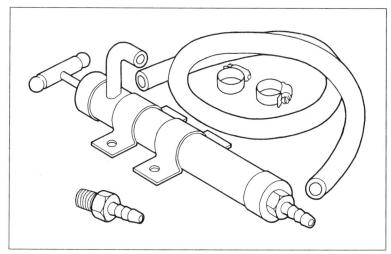

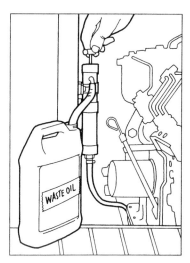

DISPOSING OF OIL

We are all aware of the effects of oil spills on our fragile environment. Always dispose of used oil responsibly. Many service stations offer a collection point for recycling. *Never* pump it over the side.

ADDING USED OIL TO THE FUEL

Operators of truck fleets sometimes dispose of large quantities of dirty oil in this way. It is technically possible to mix oil into diesel—as much as 17% by volume—but it requires filtration to remove contaminants and an expensive homogenization rig to mix the oil thoroughly. Clearly, this is not a practical proposition, even for the long-term cruiser.

OIL PUMP

Most oil pumps use an epicycloidal design, turning a multi-lobed rotor within a rotating body that has one more slot than the rotor has lobes. The pump sucks oil out of the oil pan, or sump, and pumps it through the oil filter and into internal galleries that feed the bearing surfaces. Oil pumps are maintenance free and rarely give problems.

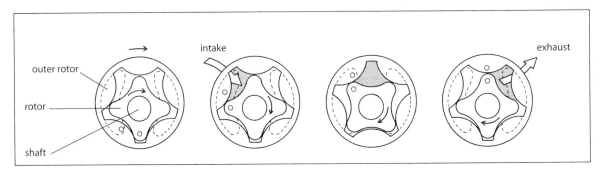

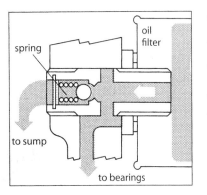

OIL PRESSURE–REGULATING VALVE

The pressure-regulating valve is a simple ball valve kept on a seat by a spring. When oil pressure reaches a preset value, the ball lifts off the seat and bleeds excess oil back to the oil pan. Pressure-regulating valves can be part of the oil pump, part of the oil-filter housing, or fitted separately. Like the oil pump, this component requires no maintenance and is relatively trouble free.

OIL FILTER

Disposable screw-on or spin-on filters are now almost universal. They are more effective than a simple sump gauze, and easier to replace than the old canister type with replaceable elements. Spin-on filters have an internal safety valve, which allows unfiltered oil to reach the bearings should the filter clog.

Always change the oil filter when you change the oil. Although the filter may have more life, it's pointless to fill the oil pan with clean oil, when a sludge-filled filter will contaminate it the next time you run the engine.

REMOVING THE FILTER

Removal is relatively simple, if somewhat messy—especially with filters mounted horizontally or upside down. Use oil-absorbent pads, rags, or a container to catch any spills. Various filter-wrench designs are available from automotive stores; the cloth-strap type works well over a wide range of filter sizes. If you don't have a wrench, punch a screwdriver midway through the old filter for better leverage.

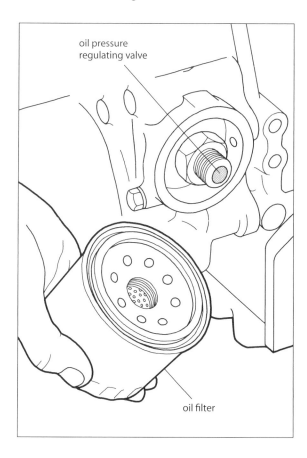

oil pressure regulating valve

oil filter

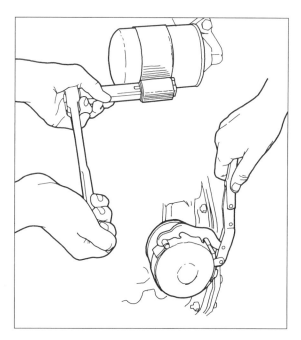

FITTING A NEW FILTER

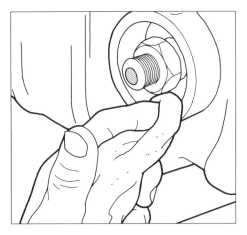

1. Wipe the contact sealing surfaces clean.

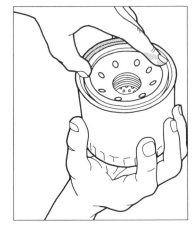

2. Lightly smear the filter seal with clean oil to improve sealing and ease removal for the next time.

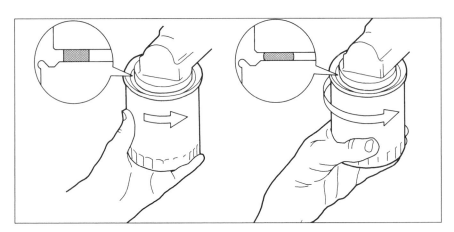

3. Spin on the filter until the seal makes contact, then tighten another three-quarter turn.

PRIMING THE OIL SYSTEM

Most engine wear occurs during the first few seconds after starting, before oil reaches the bearing surfaces. This is especially so after an oil and filter change, when the filter and oil galleries are empty; in that case, it may take 30 seconds for oil to reach the crankshaft. Larger commercial engines solve this problem with an electrical high-pressure priming pump that builds up oil pressure before the engine is started.

This type of pump is less common on smaller diesels, so it's a good idea to prime the oil system after an oil and filter change. Pull the stop cable or disconnect the run solenoid to prevent the engine from firing. Then, turn the engine over on the starter until the oil pressure light extinguishes, or oil pressure shows on the gauge. Let the starter rest; then repeat the exercise once more.

OIL CONTAMINATION

Running an engine with contaminated oil can seriously damage or even destroy it in a very short time. You may not notice oil contamination until the problem is severe, and then you may have to strip the engine completely to gauge the extent of the damage. It's best to find the contamination early, determine and rectify the cause, and then clean the system thoroughly as soon as possible. Check Chapter 2, Chart 4 (Oil Problems) for possible causes of contamination.

If bearing surfaces have been damaged, you may notice an increase in oil consumption, blue exhaust smoke, or difficult starting (piston rings and cylinders); screeching (rings and cylinders or other bearings); low oil pressure (main bearings); and hard mechanical knocking (rod bearings).

RAW WATER OR COOLANT IN THE OIL

Water will usually show on the dipstick as clear droplets in the oil, and the engine will appear to be "making oil" as the sump level increases. If the engine has been running, the oil will appear thick, gray, and milky; otherwise, the heavier water will separate and settle below the oil. If you can't see water in the oil, drain some oil into a glass container and let it settle overnight. Colored coolant will become quite visible if present.

Water—particularly salt water—can severely damage bearing surfaces, especially if it has been present for more than a few hours.

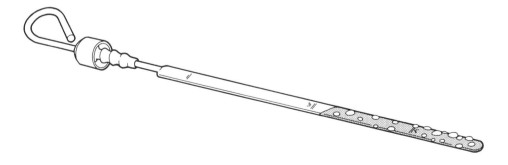

METAL IN THE OIL

Minute quantities of metal from bearing surfaces are produced in normal wear and usually remain invisible to the naked eye. If you do notice metal particles when the sump is drained, it pays to look further for the cause.

If you're concerned with the quantity or size of particles, cut open the oil filter with tin snips (a hacksaw will just deposit more metal) and wash the outside of the paper element with solvent into a container. Use a magnet to separate ferrous metals from the solution; then drain the remainder through a coffee filter to collect the debris.

Assessing the source of metal and degree of wear is not an easy task. As a rough guide, if the metal particles you collect from a small diesel fill more than 1/100 of a teaspoon, or if individual particles are larger than a coarse grain of sand, call in expert help.

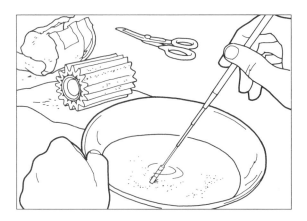

FUEL IN THE OIL

Diesel is not a good lubricant; running an engine for any length of time with fuel-diluted oil can seriously damage main and rod bearings. Look for thin oil with a strong diesel smell. The engine will appear to be "making oil," with the level on the dipstick slowly rising. A split or hole in the fuel lift-pump diaphragm is a common culprit.

SLUDGE IN THE OIL

If the oil is exceptionally thick and dark, it is most likely due to heavy contamination through infrequent changes or low-quality oil. Small quantities of antifreeze in the oil also cause sludge.

THIN OIL

If you don't smell diesel, the oil is probably well used and filled with contaminants affecting viscosity. Try replacing the oil more frequently, but continue to monitor the level, just in case there is diesel in the oil.

OIL ANALYSIS

If you suspect contamination but cannot identify the source, most oil manufacturers offer a spectromatic oil analysis service that will accurately measure the type and amount of contaminants in suspension. This service is intended more for larger operators monitoring the wear cycle of fleet engines, but is also available to the small diesel owner. Oil analysis is particularly effective in comparing samples from the same engine over time.

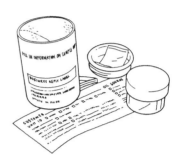

CLEANING A CONTAMINATED OIL SYSTEM

If you discover oil contamination, drain the oil, eliminate the source of contamination, and clean the system as soon as possible. Clean and run the engine promptly if you discover raw water or coolant in the oil, before any residue has a chance to corrode and seize rings in the cylinder bores.

1. Close the seacock and remove the raw-water pump impeller.

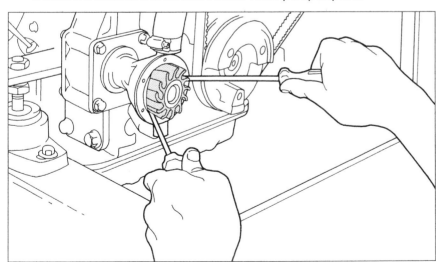

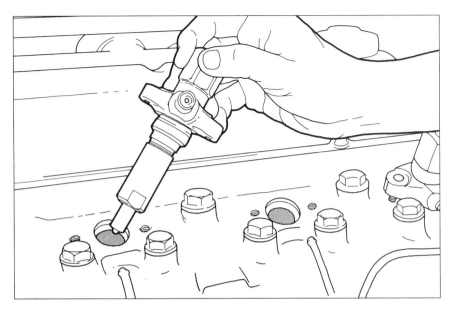

2. Remove all the injectors and turn the engine over by hand several times to expel any fluid from the cylinders.
3. Drain the sump. Replace the oil and oil filter.

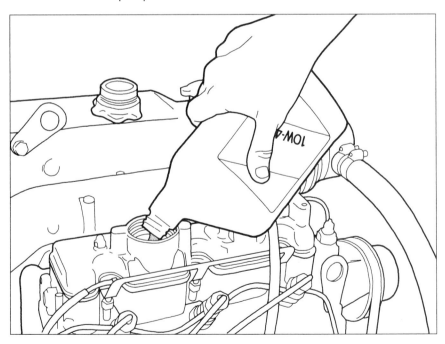

4. With the stop lever pulled out, or while pressing the stop button, turn the engine over using the starter until oil pressure shows on the gauge or the oil warning light goes out.

5. Repeat several times to circulate oil to all the components. Do not overload the starter—if it's too hot to touch, let it cool for 30 minutes.

6. Replace the oil and filter again, checking the color of the oil. If it's still contaminated, repeat steps 5 and 6 until the oil looks clean.

7. Refit the injectors and raw-water pump impeller. Open the seacock. Start the engine and run for five minutes.

8. Change the oil and replace the filter once more. Run the engine for 30 minutes to achieve operating temperature, then change the oil and filter once again.

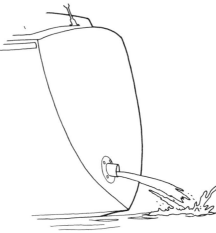

This process should remove all traces of contamination. With luck, there was minimal damage to the bearing surfaces. Double the frequency of the next two oil changes and monitor the oil gauge closely; low pressures indicating bearing damage.

LUBRICATION SYSTEM FAULTS

Problem	Possible Cause	Possible Symptoms
PICKUP TUBE		
Filter screen blocked	Oil contaminated [5]	Erratic, low, or no oil pressure
Tube defective	Seals defective [4] Tube loose [5]	As above
OIL PUMP		
Worn	Normal wear—high hours [4]	Low oil pressures
Drive loose	Poor assembly [5]	As above
PRESSURE-RELIEF VALVE		
Worn	Normal wear—high hours [4]	Low oil pressures
Sticking	Contamination [3] Wear [4]	Erratic pressures
Incorrect pressure	Incorrect setting [4] Spring worn or tired [4]	Stable pressures outside of limits
OIL FILTER		
External leaks	Filter loose [2] Seal dirty or damaged [2] Incorrect filter [3]	
OIL		
Level low	Poor maintenance [1] High consumption [2] External leaks [3]	Low or erratic oil pressures
Level high	Poor maintenance [1] Contamination with coolant, water, or fuel—see below	Increased external leakage; excessive exhaust smoke; engine over-revs out of control
Contaminated	See Troubleshooting Chart 4	
High consumption	Excessive wear [3]	Consistently low oil levels; excessive blue exhaust smoke

Problem	Possible Cause	Possible Symptoms
CRANKCASE PRESSURE		
High	Blocked breather [3] Worn piston rings and cylinders [3]	High oil consumption; blue exhaust smoke; difficult starting; increased external leakage; engine over-revs out of control
CRANKSHAFT OIL SEALS		
Leaking	High oil level [2]	Excessive crankcase pressure; possible blue exhaust smoke
	Worn or damaged seal [3]	External oil leak; oil will drip from flywheel housing if rear seal is defective
	Excessive crankcase pressure [3]	High oil mist from crankcase breather will cause blue exhaust smoke if breather connected to inlet
	Excessive wear on main bearings [4]	If bearings are worn enough to allow crankshaft to move, the engine is very tired and should be knocking from bottom end
	Scored or worn crankshaft [4]	External oil leak; oil will drip from flywheel housing if rear seal is defective

HOW LIKELY?   [1] Very common   [2] Common   [3] Possible   [4] Rare   [5] Very rare

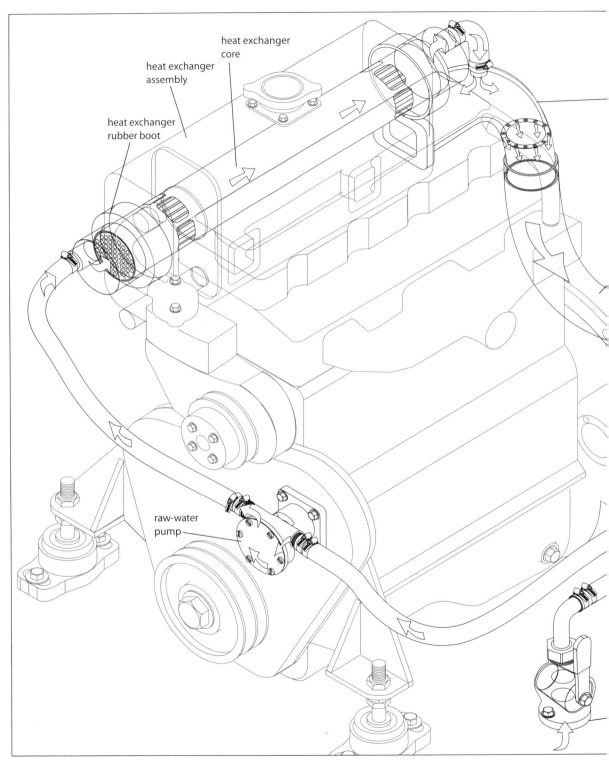

heat exchanger core

heat exchanger assembly

heat exchanger rubber boot

raw-water pump

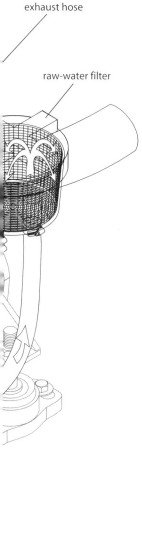

exhaust injection elbow

exhaust hose

raw-water filter

raw-water inlet
shutoff valve

5

THE RAW-WATER CIRCUIT

When diesel fuel is burned in the cylinders, roughly 30% of the heat energy is converted to usable power, 35% disappears with the exhaust gases, and 35% remains as excess heat that would melt the engine if it weren't quickly removed. The marine engine dissipates surplus heat into raw cooling water that is pumped through the engine and then overboard by way of the exhaust.

A marine diesel can be either direct cooled or indirect cooled.

On a direct-cooled engine, a raw-water pump circulates raw water through the engine block and cylinder head, out through the exhaust manifold, into the exhaust injection manifold, and overboard through the wet exhaust. A thermostat maintains engine temperature by controlling the amount of cooling water that bypasses the engine. Direct-cooled engines have lower-temperature thermostats to reduce salt formation.

The advantages of direct-cooled engines are their simplicity, lower cost, and reduced bulk. The disadvantage, though, is their vulnerability to corrosion—particularly with smaller, inexpensive automotive engines that have been marinized.

Indirect-cooled engines route the raw water through a heat exchanger, where it extracts surplus heat from the engine coolant. The raw water is then pumped into the injection elbow and overboard through the wet exhaust.

Because only the raw-water pump and heat exchanger come into contact with raw water, corrosion problems on indirect-cooled engines are reduced. This type of engine may cost more, but its longer life makes it worth every cent.

The raw-water circuit requires regular maintenance to keep the pump working and waterways clear of debris, salt deposits, and corrosion. Most overheating problems can be traced to poor maintenance of the cooling circuits.

THROUGH-HULL FITTING AND VALVE

INSPECTION

Check for leaks, corrosion, and good sealing. The valve must operate easily, but depending on type it may require a locking screw to be loosened first. Some composite valves require part of the body to be unscrewed before the valve will turn. Never force a tight valve while the boat is in the water.

RAW-WATER STRAINER

A raw-water strainer keeps debris from damaging the raw-water impeller or obstructing cooling-water flow. It must be an adequate size for the job.

INSPECTION

Close the seacock. Remove any debris from the basket. Check gaskets and seals for leaks. Check for corrosion, particularly on wing nuts that hold covers in place. Plastic strainers tend to be maintenance free, but hose connections are easily split by over-tightening the hose clamps. Remember to open the seacock on completion.

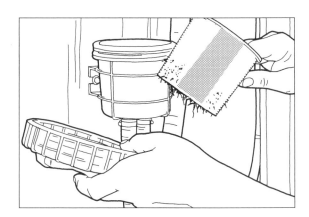

RECONDITIONING

1. Close seacock.
2. Disconnect the hoses and remove the filter from the boat.
3. Disassemble the filter.

4. Sandblast metal components if possible, or dip them in a 25% solution of muriatic acid. Dip for the minimum time; prolonged contact will damage brass or bronze. Muriatic acid works well on plastic bowls. (Do not scrape or use solvents on plastics.) Wash parts thoroughly with water to remove all traces of acid.
5. Replace the seals and gaskets. Replacement kits are available for most brands.
6. Reassemble and reinstall, checking the hoses and hose clamps.
7. Replace the anodes. (See Chapter 5 for information on anodes.)
8. Spray all metal with a heavy-duty corrosion inhibitor.

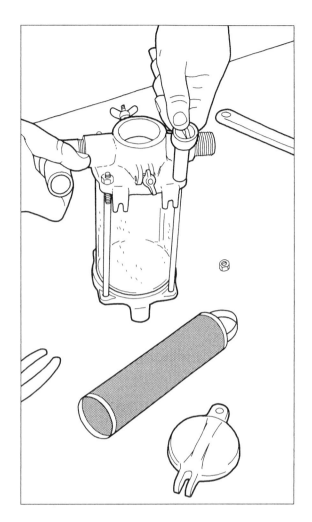

RAW-WATER PUMP

Raw-water pumps continuously suck cooling water from outside the boat and pump it through the engine. Nearly all small-diesel raw-water pumps contain rubber-vaned impellers. These self-priming pumps give good service if well installed and maintained, despite each vane's flexing more than a million times in every 10 engine hours. The weak point of these pumps is the vulnerability of the soft rubber impeller: hard debris or loss of lubricating water can destroy them in seconds. With an adequate water supply and a good strainer upstream, the average impeller should give a couple of seasons' service—provided it does not have to work against high suction or pressure.

INSPECTION

Check the front cover gasket for leaks. Corroded cover screws are common, often severe enough for heads to be missing. Check the pump body drain hole for raw water or oil, a sure sign of shaft seal failure. Water flow from the exhaust outlet will give a good indication of pump condition.

REMOVING THE IMPELLER

1. Remove the screws that retain the front cover and remove the cover plate and gasket.

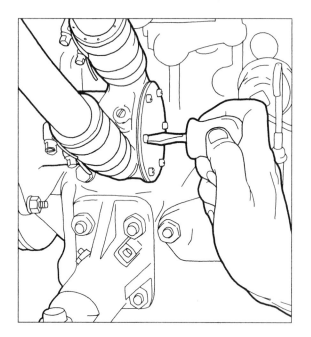

2. Pry out the small rubber plug that protects the impeller splines, if fitted.

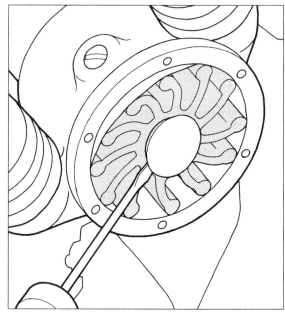

3. Check the way in which the impeller is attached to the pump shaft. Most pumps have splined impellers, but some have keyways and others have a through-bolt. Removing the splined impeller with pliers will usually tear the vanes; it's better to use two blunt screwdrivers as levers.

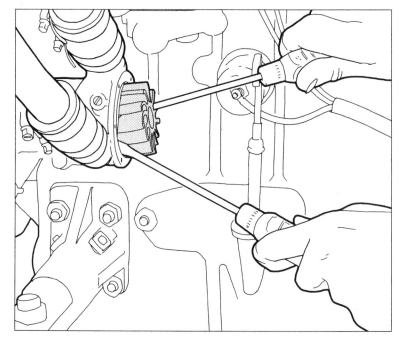

INSPECTING THE IMPELLER

Check for:

- Damaged or missing vanes. Missing vanes normally lodge themselves in the heat-exchanger inlet. Locate and remove them.
- Permanent set. New vanes are perpendicular to center. A slight set is acceptable.
- Worn vanes. The tips of new vanes have a symmetrical bead. Tips will wear on one side.
- Hardening of the rubber with age.
- Corrosion of the cover plate screws.
- Scoring of the cover plate, which dramatically reduces pump efficiency.

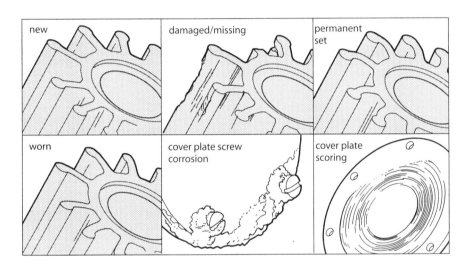

INSTALLING THE IMPELLER

- When refitting the impeller, lubricate it with lithium grease if you plan to run the pump soon; otherwise, use a silicone grease or prime with water. Don't forget the impeller plug, if fitted.
- Install used impellers with the same direction of rotation as before.
- Where an O-ring is used to seal the front cover, lightly grease the ring. O-rings can be reused if supple and not damaged.
- Where a paper gasket is used to seal the cover, clean the sealing faces with solvent to remove surplus grease. Always fit a new paper gasket. A flexible sealant works well here.

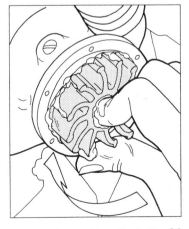

RECONDITIONING A RAW-WATER PUMP

Reconditioning a raw-water pump can be costly. Often the pump body, shaft, and drive gear are the only reuseable parts. Professional reconditioning may not be economical if the pump shaft needs replacing.

DISASSEMBLING THE PUMP

Pump designs vary widely—even within the same manufacturer's product line. The following instructions will work with most designs, but proceed with care in case your pump calls for special procedures.

1. Remove the front cover plate and the impeller (see above).

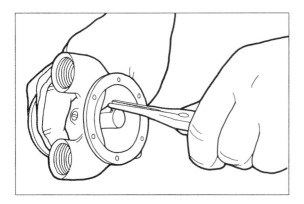

2. If the impeller is secured with a key, remove the key.

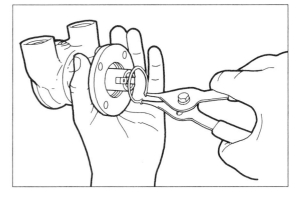

4. Remove the bearing-retaining snap ring(s), if fitted.

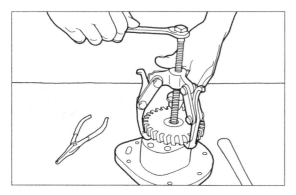

3. Remove the drive gear. Pumps with drive couplings can skip this step.

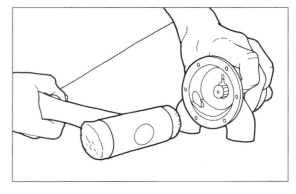

5. Tap the shaft and bearing assembly out of the pump body. Do not hammer on the shaft.

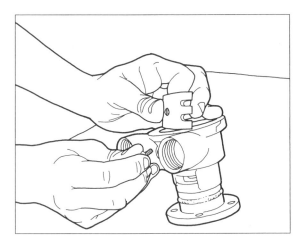

6. Remove the screw that holds the cam (if fitted). Remove the cam.

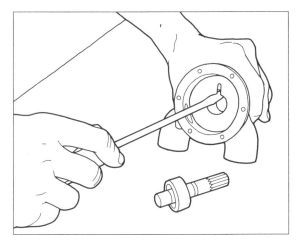

7. Remove the back plate carefully (if fitted) with a screwdriver. These thin plates can be difficult to remove without damaging them.

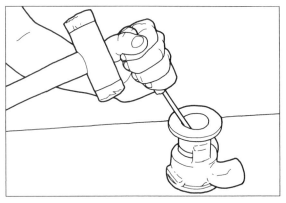

8. With a screwdriver and hammer, remove the shaft seals from the pump body. Disassembly will damage the seals—this is normal. Take care that the screwdriver blade picks up only the rear face of the seal and not the pump body, which can break.

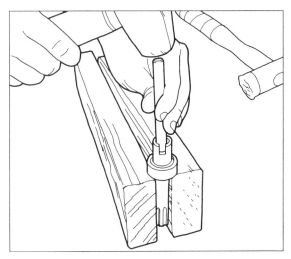

9. Remove the bearing(s) from the shaft with a puller or press. *Note*: If you must hammer on the shaft, use a soft-faced hammer or a block of wood to protect the soft stainless shaft, which distorts easily. Shafts are *very* expensive!

INSPECTING THE PUMP COMPONENTS

Pump Body. If the impeller housing is deeply scored or pitted by corrosion, go no further: You need a new pump.

Cam. Check the cam for scoring and corrosion.

Shaft. Shaft scoring where the seals rub that is deep enough to be felt with a fingernail means replacement seals will have a short life. Replace the shaft.

Bearings. Bearings are usually self-lubricating, sealed-ball races; they should feel smooth and have no play. Bearings are relatively cheap; once you've stripped the pump this far, you may as well replace them.

Cover plate and back plate. Replace the cover plate and/or back plate if either shows significant scoring.

Screws. Cover plate and cam screws are particularly vulnerable to corrosion. If pink, replace. (See page 93 for more on pink corrosion.)

Seals. Replace.

Impeller. Replace.

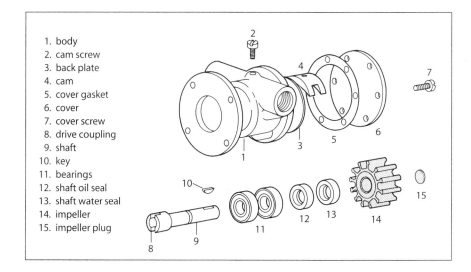

1. body
2. cam screw
3. back plate
4. cam
5. cover gasket
6. cover
7. cover screw
8. drive coupling
9. shaft
10. key
11. bearings
12. shaft oil seal
13. shaft water seal
14. impeller
15. impeller plug

REBUILDING

To reassemble the pump, reverse the order of the above procedure, noting the following points:

- Fit the seals squarely in the body, with the springs toward the fluid it is retaining: The oil-seal spring faces the bearings, and the water-seal spring faces the impeller.
- Liberally coat the seals, shaft, and bearings with grease. Don't forget to install the rubber-washer fluid slinger, if fitted.

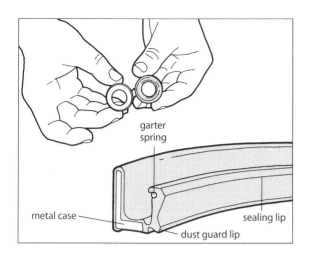

garter spring

metal case — sealing lip

dust guard lip

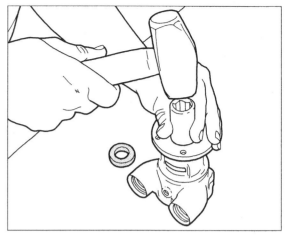

HEAT EXCHANGERS AND OIL COOLERS

Heat exchangers and oil coolers remove surplus heat from the engine. Comparing the temperatures of the raw-water inlet and outlet pipes will give a good indication of heat transfer. The inlet pipe should be slightly above ambient water temperature, and the outlet should feel *warm*. If the outlet feels *hot*, too little water is passing through the heat exchanger; check the raw-water pump, strainer, and exhaust injection elbow. If the outlet feels *cold*, water flow is good but heat transfer is poor; check the internal cleanliness of the heat exchanger's raw-water and coolant passages.

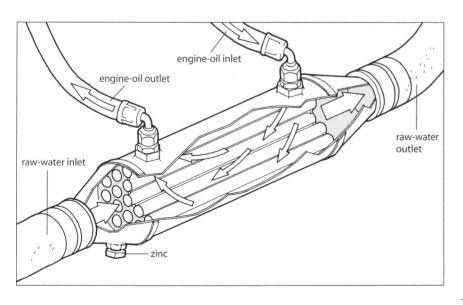

engine-oil inlet

engine-oil outlet

raw-water inlet

raw-water outlet

zinc

Salt buildup can quickly clog the raw-water side of heat exchangers and oil coolers, especially in warmer climates. The coolant side will deteriorate equally quickly if the coolant lacks corrosion inhibitors. Salt buildup dramatically affects the transfer of heat between raw water and coolant, and is a major cause of engine overheating.

Note: Shutting down a hot engine that has been working hard can cause the raw water in the heat exchanger to boil and leave heavy salt deposits. Idle the engine for 15 minutes before shutting it down.

An internal leak in a heat exchanger will result in a loss of coolant or contaminate the coolant with salt water, depending upon system pressures. An internal leak in an oil cooler can be disastrous.

CLEANING

The best way to clean heat-exchanger and oil-cooler cores is to boil the whole assembly in a noncaustic solution. If you don't have access to this type of professional-grade equipment, you can use a 25% solution of muriatic acid. But, beware: Acid-cleaning will quickly weaken a cooler, opening small holes and cracks that salts and corrosion had sealed.

If you acid-clean a core, note the following points:

- Don't forget the protective gloves and glasses!
- Immerse the core for the minimum time (just until all contamination is gone), or the corrosive acid may eat into the metal and cause serious damage.
- Cores fitted with aluminum sleeves need the special attention of a non-caustic solution; muriatic acid quickly attacks aluminum.
- Acid will contaminate the oil system, so block off oil connections on oil coolers.
- Flush the cleaned core thoroughly with water to remove all traces of acid.
- Look over the core carefully. Corrosion will show as soft, crumbly, pink metal.
- Spray the core with a light corrosion inhibitor if it won't be installed immediately.

TESTING

Test a heat exchanger by pressurizing the raw-water side with air while the whole assembly is immersed in a large container of water. Bubbles will signal a leak. An oil cooler should be pressurized on its oil side. Test pressures should be approximately 25% above specified system pressure.

Take care not to overpressurize:

- Heat exchanger with 7-lb. pressure cap—test at 10 psi
- Heat exchanger with 15-lb. pressure cap—test at 20 psi
- Engine-oil coolers running at 60 psi—test at 75 psi

Repairs are not recommended unless you are an expert coppersmith! If in doubt, always replace.

SACRIFICIAL ANODES, OR "ZINCS"

To reduce corrosion, sacrificial anodes—also called zincs—are often fitted to the raw-water side of engine components such as heat exchangers and oil coolers and to the base of most metal raw-water strainers. A direct-cooled engine will have a large zinc in the block itself.

Well-maintained zincs extend the life of the heat exchangers and oil coolers, saving your hard-earned dollars for better purposes. The frequency of zinc replacement depends on several factors, so check the zincs monthly at first to understand how long individual zincs last in your system.

CHECKING AND REPLACING

1. Remove *all* the old zinc. Pieces of old zincs can restrict heat exchangers and coolers.

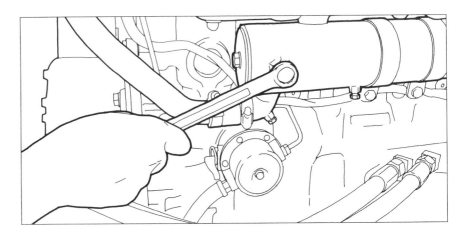

2. Knock off flaky oxides with a hammer.

3. If a zinc is less than half its original size, replace it. Tighten the new zinc well into the holder without shearing off the soft metal.

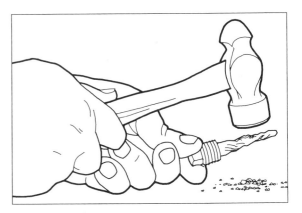

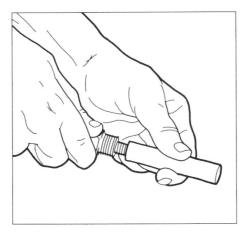

4. A flexible sealer on the plug threads will prevent leakage but still allow part of the thread to make electrical contact when tightened. Teflon tape will stop leakage, but may also prevent continuity. If in doubt, check it with a multimeter.

ANTISIPHON VALVE

The antisiphon valve prevents raw water from siphoning back into the exhaust manifold and filling the cylinders. It may be fitted between the raw-water pump and the heat exchanger or between the heat exchanger and the exhaust injection elbow. The antisiphon valve must be located at least 18 inches above the waterline to allow for heel. It may be excluded from the raw-water circuit only if the injection elbow is well above the waterline—again, under all sea conditions and angles of heel. Chapter 8 contains additional information on exhaust injection elbows.

CHECKING OPERATION

The antisiphon valve is a simple inverted U-tube with a non-return valve that prevents the pressurized raw water from escaping while the engine is running, but allows air to enter and break the siphon as soon as the engine is shut down. Check by removing the non-return valve and blowing through it in each direction. You can often resurrect defective valves by removing salt deposits with warm, soapy water.

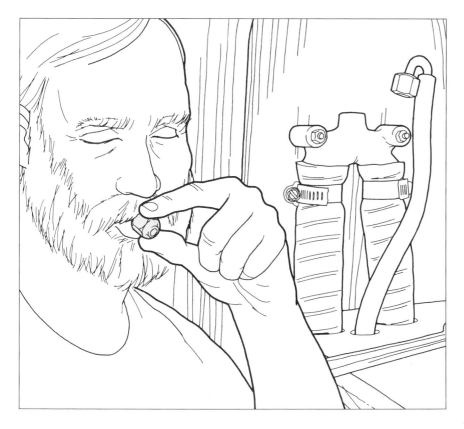

RAW-WATER HOSES

Raw-water hoses from the inlet through-hull to the strainer and on to the raw-water pump must be wire reinforced to prevent collapse under pump suction. The hoses beyond the pump are pressurized, so unreinforced hose will do the job unless a tight radius causes the hose to kink. Always use rubber hose; plastic hose does not withstand heat well.

HOSE CLAMPS

The average sailboat diesel uses dozens of hose clamps. There are many design variations, all based on a worm screw tightening a gear-cut band.

SELECTING THE CORRECT TYPE

Use only 100%–stainless hose clamps intended for marine applications. The lower grades of steel in many automotive clamps will corrode into a solid, unusable block in a very short time.

   Of the quality stainless clamps available, solid bands are far superior to slotted bands. Not only are they stronger, but they will withstand considerably more corrosion before failing.

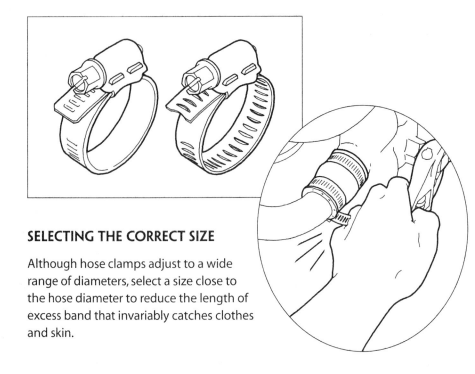

SELECTING THE CORRECT SIZE

Although hose clamps adjust to a wide range of diameters, select a size close to the hose diameter to reduce the length of excess band that invariably catches clothes and skin.

PROTECTING HOSE CLAMPS

Hose clamps are often hidden away in seldom-visited, damp corners and are often subject to extreme temperatures, humidity, and salt. Spraying each hose clamp—particularly the adjusting mechanism—with heavy-duty corrosion inhibitor will more than double its life. Repeat every time the clamp is disturbed.

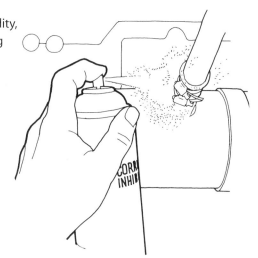

RAW-WATER THERMOSTATS

Thermostats in direct raw-water–cooled engines open at lower temperatures than those in indirect-cooled engines—usually 120°F–140°F (49°C–60°C). The instructions for inspecting and testing thermostats in Chapter 6 apply to thermostats in both direct- and indirect-cooled engines.

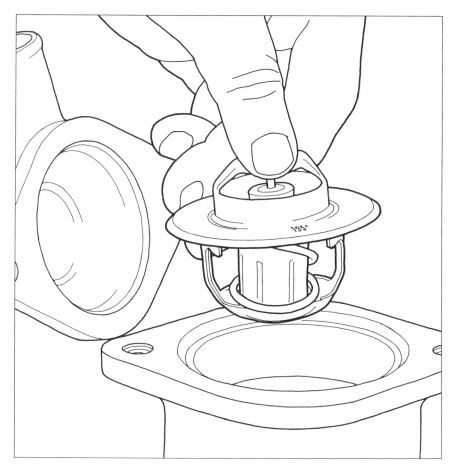

RAW-WATER CIRCUIT FAULTS

Problem	Possible Cause	Possible Symptoms

SYSTEM TEMPERATURE PROBLEMS—See Troubleshooting Chart 6, page 34

RAW-WATER STRAINER

Problem	Possible Cause	Possible Symptoms
Restricted	Contaminated with debris [2]	Insufficient raw-water flow; engine overheats
Leaking	Gaskets defective [2] Cover loose [2] Hose clamps loose [3]	External raw-water leaks; if strainer is above waterline, air will be sucked into cooling system; engine overheats

RAW-WATER PUMP

Problem	Possible Cause	Possible Symptoms
Cover plate leaking	Defective gasket [2] Screws not tight enough [3]	Visible raw-water leaks; corrosion and salt crystals are often the first sign
Water leak from pump body	Shaft water seal defective [2] Shaft worn [2]	As above
Oil leaking from pump body	Shaft oil seal defective [3] Shaft worn [3] Excessive crankcase pressure [4]	Visible oil leak
Pump body hot	No water flow [1] Through-hull closed [1] Strainer blocked [1] Air leak on inlet side of pump [3]	High operating temperature; engine overheats
Poor pumping	Defective impeller [1] Worn or rough body, cover plate, cam, or back plate [2] High exhaust backpressure [3] Excessive suction—pump too high above waterline [3] Inadequate water supply—see above	As above
Impeller torn	Debris passing through pump [1] Pump overloaded [3] High exhaust backpressure [3] Excessive suction—pump too high above waterline [3]	As above
Impellers failing often	Worn and rough body, cover plate, or back plate [2] Poor water supply [2] No lubrication on initial build [3] High exhaust backpressure [3] Excessive suction—pump too high above waterline [3]	As above

Problem	Possible Cause	Possible Symptoms

HEAT EXCHANGER/OIL COOLER

Problem	Possible Cause	Possible Symptoms
Corrosion	No zinc in raw-water side [1] Poor maintenance [1]	Metal "dezincified"; looks "pink," especially after cleaning
External leaks	Defective gaskets or seals [1] Loose hose clamps [2] Corroded housing or end caps [2]	Visible leaks
Internal leaks	Corrosion [2] Solder failure [4]	Heat Exchanger: Header tank "makes water"; loss of coolant Oil Cooler: See warning in chapter text.

EXHAUST INJECTION ELBOW—See Chapter 8

DIRECT-COOLING THERMOSTAT—See Chapter 8 (For coolant-system thermostat, the symptoms are the same.)

HOW LIKELY?   [1] Very common   [2] Common   [3] Possible   [4] Rare   [5] Very rare

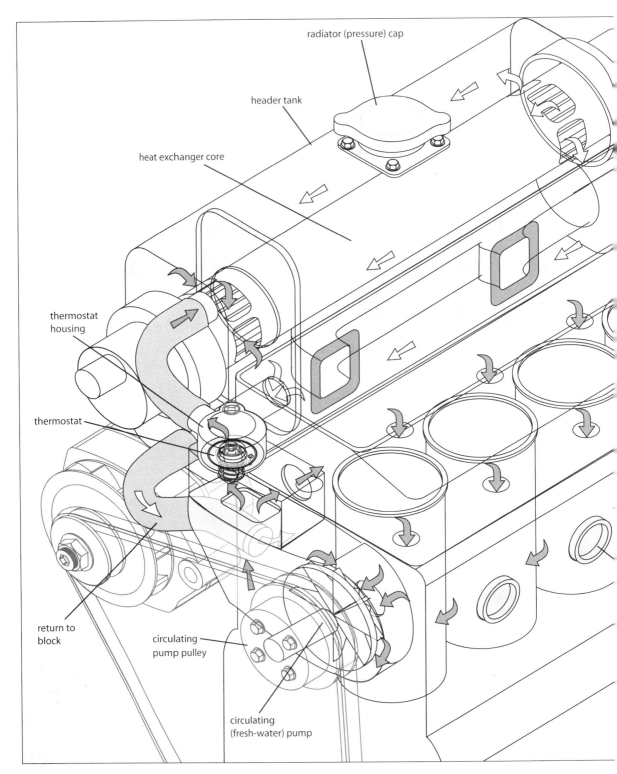

radiator (pressure) cap

header tank

heat exchanger core

thermostat housing

thermostat

return to block

circulating pump pulley

circulating (fresh-water) pump

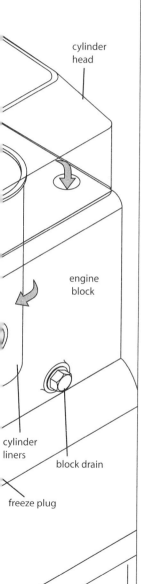

xhaust manifold

cylinder
head

engine
block

cylinder
liners

block drain

freeze plug

6

THE COOLANT CIRCUIT

The majority of boats are equipped with indirect-cooled diesels, in which a freshwater or coolant circuit keeps corrosive raw water away from the main-engine components.

A dedicated, belt-driven centrifugal pump circulates coolant through the engine block and cylinder head to remove surplus heat. The hot coolant then passes through a heat exchanger, where the heat transfers to the raw-water circuit and is pumped overboard with the raw water through the exhaust. A thermostat maintains the temperature of the engine by controlling coolant flow through the block and cylinder head.

Coolant circuits require regular maintenance to keep the components clean and to ensure good heat transfer across the heat exchanger to the raw-water circuit. While most overheating problems can be traced to the raw-water side of the cooling system, thermostats and circulating pumps occasionally fail.

COOLANT

Keep the fresh-water circuit clean. Good-quality coolant will help prevent buildup of scale and corrosion that can reduce heat transfer by as much as 95%.

Note: Never check the coolant while the engine is hot. Removing the pressure cap from a hot engine can spray scalding water over the engine bay. Always wait until the engine has cooled to below 120°F (48.9°C) or feels warm to the touch.

INSPECTION

Check the coolant level before you start the engine. The coolant should be visible. Where access is poor, you should be able to feel the level with your finger. An adequate mix will have a strong coolant-green/blue color. (Simple hydrometers are available to measure mixtures more accurately.) Internal corrosion and overheating are indicated by brown discoloration.

WHICH COOLANT?

Coolant added to water will lower the freezing point and raise the boiling point; and prevent corrosion. Most coolants are based on ethylene glycol (although the heavier-duty varieties use propylene glycol), and contain additives to reduce foaming, corrosion, and scale deposits. Good-quality coolants will give the best protection.

WHAT MIXTURE?

Mix coolant and water in a 50/50 solution. Any lower concentration of coolant will reduce both corrosion and freeze protection. A mixture of more than 70% coolant will gel and block waterways, causing overheating.

COOLANT MIXTURE VERSUS TEMPERATURE PROTECTION

Antifreeze Concentration By Volume (%)	Propylene Glycol	Ethylene Glycol
	Freeze Point (°F)	
0	32	32
20	19	16
30	10	4
40	-6	-12
50	-27	-34
60	-56	-62
80	-71	-57
100	-76	-5

DRAINING THE OLD COOLANT

The location of coolant drains differs with each engine.

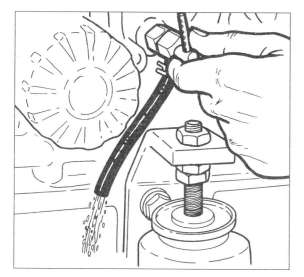

Engine block — usually aft, above the height of the crankshaft.

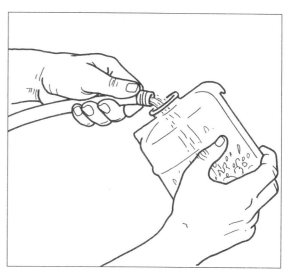

Expansion tank (if fitted) — remove the tank and wash it out.

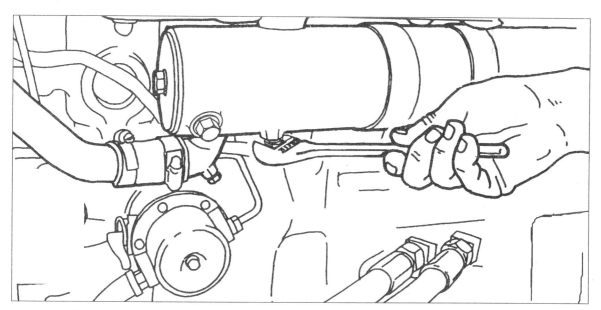

Header tank — probably will drain through the cylinder block, but some engines have separate drains.

Heat exchanger — at the lowest point.

CLEANING THE COOLANT CIRCUIT

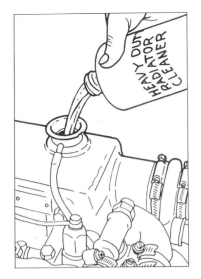

An acid-based solution will remove scale and corrosion. Acid will also find weak points, so if your heat exchanger or header tank has been neglected, acid-cleaning will find their faults.

Automotive stores carry several types of acid-based radiator cleaners; select the strongest one. These products are simple to use, but always follow the instructions on the bottle.

ADDING COOLANT

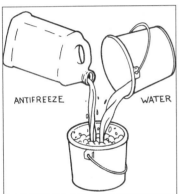

Premix the coolant to the proper concentration in a separate container. Pour the solution into the correct filler cap—it's not an unusual mistake to pour coolant into the oil filler. To ensure the thermostat has opened, run the engine at idle with the pressure cap off until the engine reaches operating temperature. Continue adding more solution until the header tank is full. Top off the expansion tank, if fitted.

TESTING THE COOLANT CIRCUIT FOR LEAKS

If you suspect a leak in the coolant circuit or have just rebuilt any of the components, it's good practice to pressure-test the system. You'll need a coolant-pressure tester that fits on the header tank. If you don't own a tester, it may be worth borrowing one: A 10-minute check can save you the considerable time it would take to disassemble the entire system and test components individually.

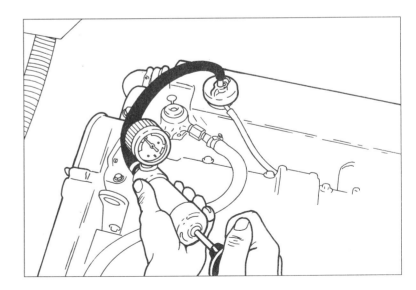

HEADER TANK

Many engines have a header tank that combines a water-cooled exhaust manifold and heat exchanger. The tank itself requires no scheduled maintenance; it is, however, usually made from cast aluminum, which is vulnerable to corrosion. White, powdery deposits under hoses and around joints are the signal to remove the header tank and treat the corrosion.

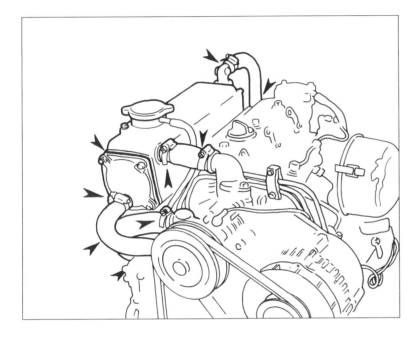

PRESSURE CAP

The pressure cap on the header tank is identical to an automotive radiator cap, and requires no scheduled maintenance. It's not unusual for corrosion to appear on the cap's external surface, but should it affect the spring or sealing surfaces, replace the cap. Replacements must have the correct pressure rating for the system—usually 7 or 15 psi.

EXPANSION TANK

Expansion, or overflow, tanks are common on automotive engines, and are sometimes found on marine engines. The tank collects the expanding coolant as the engine warms, and returns it as the engine cools, keeping the header tank full and the heat exchanger fully immersed in coolant at all times.

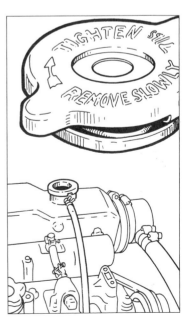

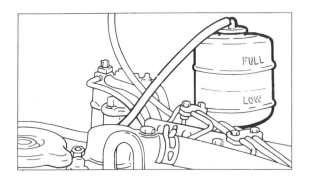

Design variations include simple expansion bottles or fully pressurized containers, which are usually constructed of translucent plastic to permit easy monitoring of the level.

Note: Don't rely on the expansion tank alone as an indicator of coolant level. Always check coolant level in the header tank. If the expansion-tank hose breaks its siphon, the header tank can show full with the engine out of water.

THERMOSTAT

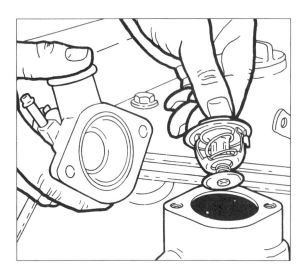

The thermostat is a simple, temperature-sensitive valve that opens and closes to control coolant flow through the engine block and cylinder head.

In operation, thermostats hover in the partially open position, sensing variations in coolant temperature caused by changing loads and ambient conditions. If a temperature gauge is fitted, the temperature should gradually rise from cold to operating temperature as the thermostat begins to control. A sticking thermostat will allow the temperature to rise well above operating temperature before it opens; or, if it is already stuck open, the engine may take a long time or never reach the correct temperature.

INSPECTION

Remove the thermostat from the engine. If it is contaminated, corroded, or shows score marks where it has been binding on its guide, replace it.

TESTING

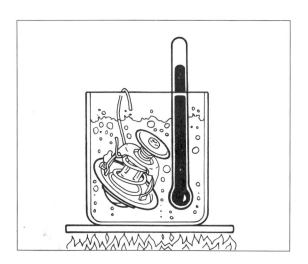

Check the rating stamped on the flange or body. At temperatures below this rating, the thermostat should be fully closed. Test by suspending it in a container of water and slowly bringing it to a boil. The thermostat should start to open at its rated temperature. If you don't have a thermometer, watch the thermostat open as the water approaches boiling point. It must be fully open by the time the water boils and fully closed once the water cools. If not, replace it.

CIRCULATING PUMP

Circulating pumps are mostly of the centrifugal type. Such pumps are simple in construction, with problems limited to seal leakage or bearing failure. They can often be reconditioned but usually require a hydraulic press to remove the pulley or bearings.

CHECKING SEALS

The face seals in a circulating pump keep the coolant from reaching sealed bearings. When a seal fails, coolant leaks from the pump-body drain. Leaks will be more noticeable if the engine is shut down at operating temperature, when the system is pressurized. Any leakage means that the pump should be replaced or reconditioned before the coolant causes bearing failure.

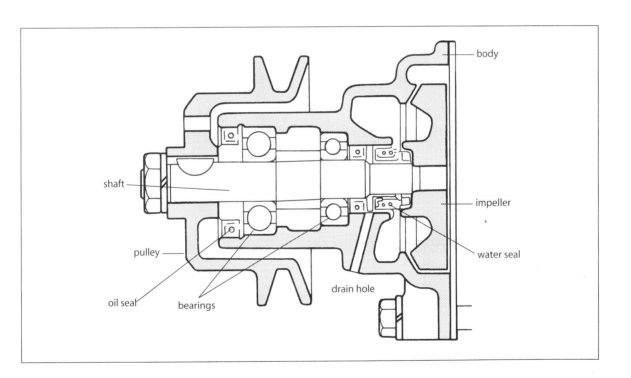

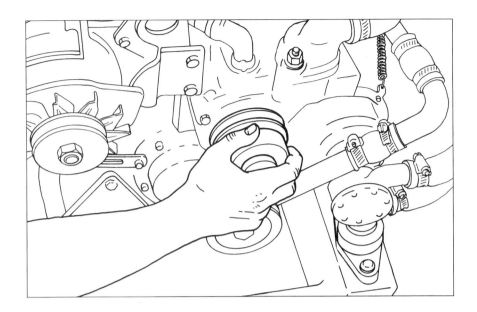

CHECKING BEARINGS

Circulating pumps usually have two self-lubricating and sealed ball race bearings. Check the bearings with the V-belt removed; they should feel smooth when rotated by hand. Grip the pulley firmly and try moving it side to side and fore and aft. Any more than negligible movement means that the bearings are close to failure; replace or recondition the pump.

V-BELT

The V-belt drives both the circulating pump and the alternator from the crankshaft pulley. If the belt fails, the circulating pump will not run, and the engine will overheat in minutes. Check the belt regularly as part of your startup routine, and always carry a spare.

INSPECTION

Check for excessive wear, cracking, and polished or sticky V surfaces. If in doubt, replace the belt. If you upgrade alternators, upgrade the belts and pulleys as well.

CORRECT TENSION

Belt tension is correct when firm thumb pressure applied midway along the longest belt run deflects the belt by about $\frac{1}{2}$ inch. Insufficient tension allows the

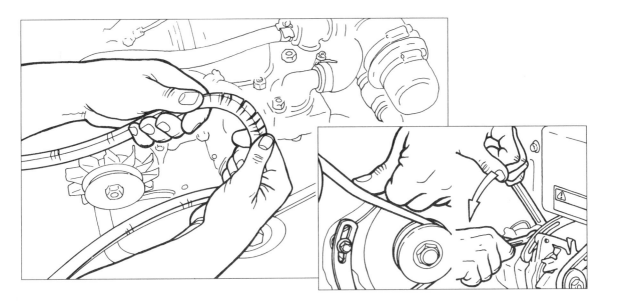

belt to slip; too much tension causes premature bearing failure in pumps and alternators. Adjust tension by repositioning the alternator.

COOLANT-CIRCUIT HOSES

Hoses used in the coolant circuit connect the circulating pump, heat exchanger, and oil cooler to the cylinder head and engine block.

INSPECTION

Coolant hoses suffer the effects of high temperature, pressure, and contact with coolant and oil. Rubber hoses should feel soft when squeezed. Check for bulging, splits, cracking, chafing, and stickiness caused by oil contamination.

COOLANT CIRCUIT FAULTS

Problem	Possible Cause	Possible Symptoms

SYSTEM TEMPERATURE PROBLEMS—See Troubleshooting Chart 6, page 34

HEADER TANK

Problem	Possible Cause	Possible Symptoms
Coolant low	Natural expansion [1] External leaks [3] Internal leaks [4]	Tank needs frequent filling
Coolant dirty	Not changed often enough [2] Overheating [3]	High temperature
"Making water"	Defective heat exchanger [3] Loose hose clamps on heat exchanger rubber boots [3]	Continuous flow of water from open pressure cap or through overflow tube
Oil in coolant	Cylinder-head gasket blown [3]	As above

PRESSURE CAP

Problem	Possible Cause	Possible Symptoms
Leaking	Defective seal [3]	Excessive leak as engine warms up and pressure builds
	Cylinder-head gasket blown [3]	Excess pressure in cooling system; coolant will be blown out of cap; loss of power; poor starting

CIRCULATING PUMP

Problem	Possible Cause	Possible Symptoms
Noise	Bearing failure; probably caused by seal failure or V-belt too tight [3]	Shaft seal leaking often indicates initial deterioration
Coolant leaking from pump body	Shaft seal failure [2]	External leak; coolant low in header tank

V-BELT

Problem	Possible Cause	Possible Symptoms
Slipping	Too loose [1]	First sign: polishing of contact surfaces; squealing; overheating; low alternator output; false reading on alternator-driven tachometers

Problem	Possible Cause	Possible Symptoms
V-BELT continued		
Excessive wear	Too tight [2] Poor alignment of crankshaft, water pump, and alternator pulleys [2] Belt overstressed, often by upgrading alternator without increasing pulley and belt size [2]	Excessive wear on circulating pump and alternator bearings; large amounts of belt dust adjacent to belt track; thinning of belt
Thrown belt	Belt too loose [2] Pulleys not correctly aligned [2]	Engine overheats; alternator-driven tachometers will not work

THERMOSTAT

Problem	Possible Cause	Possible Symptoms
Stuck open	Wear [2] Contamination [2]	Normal circuit: Operating temperature remains low. Bypass-type circuit: Engine will overheat.
Stuck closed	Wear [2] Contamination [2]	Normal circuit: Operating temperature very high; engine overheats. Bypass-type circuit: Operating temperature remains low.
Thermostat not fitted	Someone tried to overcome system overheating problems incorrectly [2]	Normal circuit: Engine will not reach operating temperature. Bypass-type circuit: Engine will overheat.

HOW LIKELY?   [1] Very common   [2] Common   [3] Possible   [4] Rare   [5] Very rare

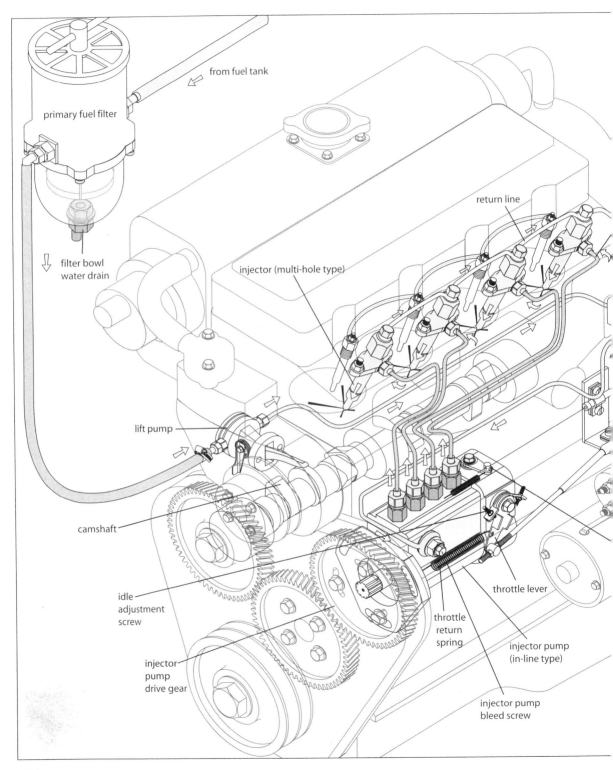

from fuel tank

primary fuel filter

filter bowl
water drain

return line

injector (multi-hole type)

lift pump

camshaft

idle
adjustment
screw

injector
pump
drive gear

throttle
return
spring

throttle lever

injector pump
(in-line type)

injector pump
bleed screw

7
THE FUEL SYSTEM

ector supply
es (pipes)

secondary fuel filter
bleed screw

return to tank

shutoff cable

throttle cable

secondary filter

water drain

shutoff valve
(mechanical)

An efficient diesel engine requires a precise amount of fuel atomized into the combustion chamber at *exactly* the right time. Injecting these minute quantities of fuel accurately at high speed and pressure demands components with mirror-smooth surfaces and fits measured in ten-thousandths of an inch. Therein lies the weakness of the diesel engine: Even the smallest particle of dirt or water can seize or corrode components. For this reason, engine manufacturers design their fuel systems with good filtration and water separation to remove all contaminants *before* they reach the injector pump or injectors.

Fuel system cleanliness is essential to keeping a diesel engine running reliably. Keep the fuel free of dirt and water, and your fuel system will give years of reliable service: Injectors will continue to atomize, and the engine will start more easily, burn less fuel, and produce less smoke.

Replace filters regularly to prevent dirt and water from restricting delivery or contaminating the system. Injector nozzles gradually wear and need periodic testing to confirm they are atomizing the fuel correctly.

Surprisingly, a diesel will run even when a defective injection system is pouring uneven quantities of neat fuel into the engine. The lax owner may not even notice the deterioration in performance until the engine eventually fails to start.

After the starting system, the fuel system is the most likely to cause problems. Common faults can be traced to contamination with air, water, and dirt and the slow deterioration of injectors.

FUEL

The diesel fuel we pour into our tanks contains more energy, has a higher flash point (and is therefore safer), and is heavier than the gasoline we pour into our cars. A diesel engine burns less fuel and gives off fewer emissions than its gasoline counterpart.

All diesel fuel contains sulfur; the amount depends on the quality of the crude oil and the refining process. During combustion, sulfur converts to corrosive acids that are absorbed by the oil. New emission regulations reduce the allowable sulfur content to less than 0.3%, but if you buy diesel in countries with less-stringent regulations, change the oil more frequently (see Chapter 4).

CLEANLINESS

Even the smallest amount of debris will score and block the finely machined surfaces of fuel-system components; cleanliness is essential.

If you're unsure of fuel quality, filter the fuel to remove water and dirt before it goes into your tank. A good fueling filter can be fairly expensive—especially if it can handle the flow rate of a typical dockside delivery pump. Cost is relative, however: The price of a filter is low compared to that of replacing the injectors and injector pump destroyed by contamination.

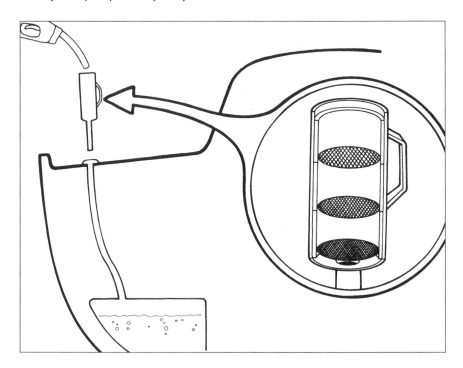

FUEL ADDITIVES

Oil companies put special additives in diesel fuel to reduce smoke, prevent pre-ignition, and mitigate the effects of low temperatures. In most cases, after-market additives have little effect, and those containing alcohol actually damage water-separator elements. There are a couple of exceptions.

Biocide. Certain types of algae and fungus survive on water in the fuel, appearing as a black, stringy sludge contaminating fuel tanks and blocking fuel lines and the primary filter. Fortunately, you can treat and even prevent such biological growth with one of several products readily available from marine-supply stores.

Fuel Lubricants. Sulfur acts as a lubricant, prolonging the life of seals and O-rings. Modern fuels with reduced sulfur may be enhanced by the addition of a fuel lubricant.

FUEL TANKS

Fuel tanks come in all shapes, sizes, and materials, depending on the boatbuilder. Although they appear to be a maintenance-free component, the accumulation of water, dirt, and debris over the years causes major problems for fuel system components. Problems usually appear when rough seas stir up the debris at the bottom of the tank—just when you need the engine most.

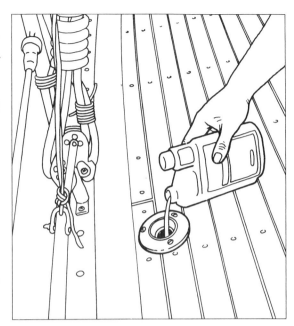

INSPECTION

Tank. Periodic opening of the inspection cover (if fitted) to clean out accumulated water and sediment is advised; frequency depends on the quality of fuel used and the tank's age and material. Inspection cover seals must be made of fuel-resistant materials. Most seals deteriorate with age, and even the best materials will eventually break up and block fuel lines. Periodically unscrew the drain plug (if fitted) to remove any water and sediment.

Tank Fittings. Check all fittings, hoses, and clamps for tightness; hoses that connect the filler to the tank are often forgotten. Pick-up tubes should reach the lowest point of the tank to prevent a buildup of water and sediment. Regularly inspect deck-mounted filler cap seals—they are a prime cause of water in the fuel. Shut-off valves should operate smoothly full travel.

PRIMARY FILTER

The primary filter provides the first and most important level of filtration. A well-designed filter will absorb considerable contamination. It *must* be capable of removing water and be of adequate size.

CHECKING THE BOWL

Inspect the filter bowl daily and drain any sediment and water. If the bowl requires draining more than once every 100 hours, the tank is dirty and needs cleaning.

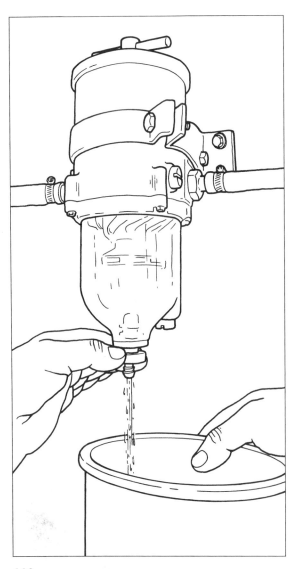

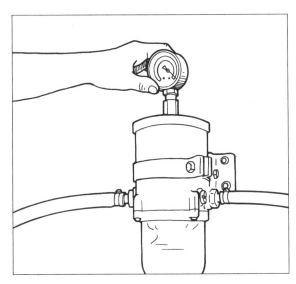

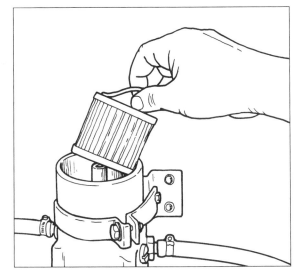

REPLACING THE ELEMENT

Replace elements at the first sign of discoloration. Always fit new seals. If replacement elements are available with different filtration rates, use the primary filter to remove the larger debris and let the secondary take care of what's left. Small engine primary filters use 10- or 20-micron elements. A vacuum gauge fitted to the outlet side of the filter can give an effective indication when the element is starting to restrict flow and needs to be replaced.

FUEL LIFT PUMP

The fuel lift pump supplies fuel under pressure to the injector pump. Most lift pumps are mechanically driven off a dedicated cam lobe on the engine camshaft. A reciprocating diaphragm sucks fuel from the fuel tank with flow controlled by two small internal non-return valves.

Lift pumps seldom have problems. Most lift pumps are sealed units that can't be repaired. Even if the pump can be stripped, repair kits can be difficult to locate; in most cases it is easier to replace the pump.

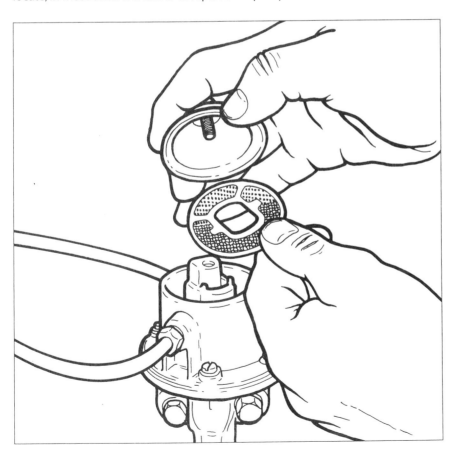

CLEANING THE PUMP FILTER SCREEN (IF ACCESSIBLE)

Clean the internal filter on fuel lift pumps annually. Remove the top cover, the seal, and the filter screen, and carefully wash the screen in a small container of diesel. Make sure the seals are good before reusing them.

CHECKING OPERATION

Disconnect the fuel outlet pipe from the pump and turn the engine over with the starter. The pump should produce full-bore flow in spurts. If it doesn't, check for supply problems by replacing the inlet pipe with a hose immersed in a container of clean diesel, and repeat the test.

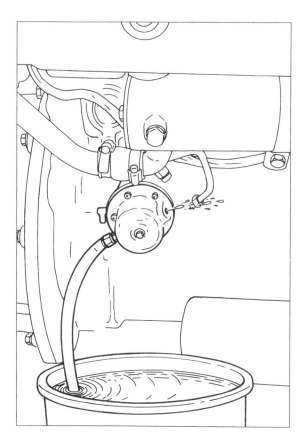

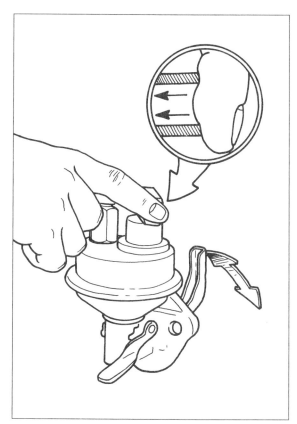

Remove a suspect pump from the engine and operate the cam lever. The pump should make a loud, sucking noise, and you should feel both suction and pressure when you place a finger over the inlet and outlet connections, respectively. (Although it's possible to test the pump on the engine using the priming lever, these levers commonly fail while the pump continues to function correctly.)

SECONDARY FUEL FILTER

The design of the secondary filter varies with engine and manufacturer. Replacement elements come in different shapes and sizes, with spin-on types becoming popular on newer engines. Each manufacturer specifies the level of filtration for their fuel system. Elements as fine as 2 microns are available that will stop particles larger than 0.002 mm (0.00008").

REPLACING THE ELEMENT

Although you don't have to replace secondary filters as often as primary filters, neglected secondary filters can still cause fuel supply problems. As a general rule, replace secondary-filter elements at every other primary-filter change.

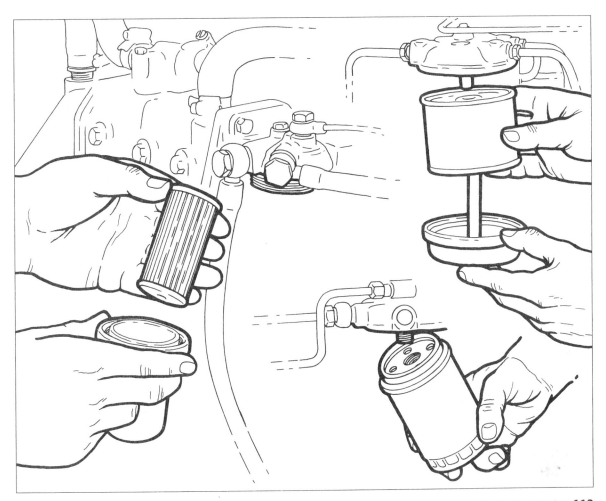

GOVERNOR

Governors are rpm–sensitive mechanisms that balance centrifuged flyweights against spring pressure to control the injector pump setting and maintain rpm under changing loads.

Governors, whether part of the engine or injector pump, require no maintenance. They may have external adjustments for maximum-rpm, acceleration, and idle-rpm settings, but only the idle-rpm setting can be altered. Maximum rpm and acceleration screws are factory set, and usually sealed; do not attempt to adjust them.

ADJUSTING IDLE RPM

Set idle rpm high enough that the engine is not laboring and shaking on its mounts, but low enough that boat speed is controllable. An incorrect idle rpm is most likely a sign of problems elsewhere. Before making adjustments, check that the injectors are atomizing well, the filters are clean, and the air supply is not restricted.

Adjust by turning the screw that sets the bottom stop of the throttle lever arm. With the engine running at operating temperature, loosen the locknut and slowly turn the stop screw in the required direction. Remember to tighten the locknut when you're satisfied with the setting.

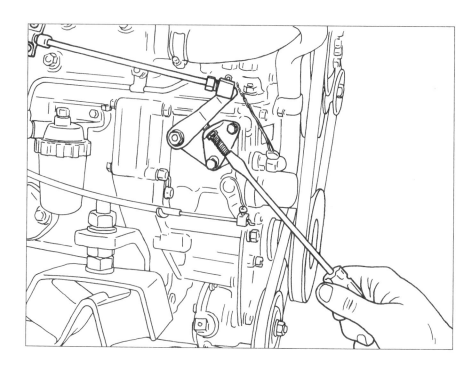

INJECTOR PUMP

The injector pump is the heart of the fuel system. This complex component receives low-pressure fuel from the lift pump, senses the engine's fuel requirement, and then, at exactly the right moment, pumps the correct amount of fuel to the injectors at very high pressure. Both in-line and distributor-type pumps are common on small diesels.

Injector pumps will provide years of reliable service if supplied with clean fuel. They are factory set and, for the most part, require no maintenance. A few models have their own oil sump and require regular oil changes. Failures are not common, and most problems are due to the presence of air.

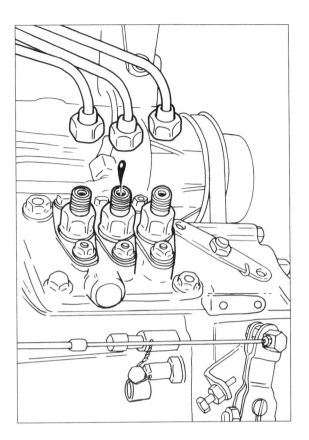

CHECKING OPERATION

If you suspect a fault with the injector pump and have confirmed that the fuel supply to the pump is good and free of air and the shut-off mechanism is not operated:

1. Remove the injector lines from the pump.
2. Turn the engine over with the starter while looking closely at the injector-line connections. You should see a small shot of fuel from each connection as the piston reaches its injection point.
3. If you don't, bleed the pump of air thoroughly and repeat the test. If the pump still fails to supply fuel, call in a more experienced mechanic before condemning an expensive pump.

FUEL TIMING

Fuel timing determines when each injector receives its shot of fuel from the injector pump. It is set by the mesh of the timing gears and the position in which the injector pump is mounted on the engine.

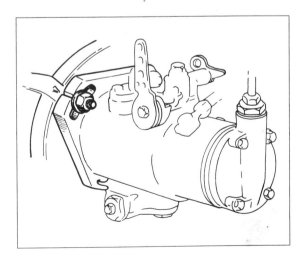

Timing varies with engine design and number of cylinders. Typically, a four-cylinder diesel will have a setting of 10° to 15° before top dead center (TDC). Timing is factory set and should not need adjustment unless the timing gears are disassembled or the injector pump disturbed. Rarely, the injector pump or timing-gear adjustment may work loose and affect the timing.

COLD-STARTING AIDS

Cold-starting aids help initial combustion by increasing combustion-air temperature and/or increasing the fuel/air ratio. Many engines will not start easily without a starting aid, even in tropical climates. The design of these devices varies.

In sub-zero temperatures, the paraffin wax in diesel fuel can separate and clog fuel lines. If you're crazy enough to play with boats in such conditions, look into purchasing heaters for the primary filter and oil sump.

THERMOSTARTS

A thermostart is an electrically heated coil that burns fuel in the intake manifold. To test, remove the intake-air filter and operate the preheat switch:

- The coil should glow.
- A flame should appear when the fuel valve opens.

If the coil doesn't heat, check power supply and grounding. If the coil glows but there is no flame, the valve may not be opening or fuel may not be reaching the device.

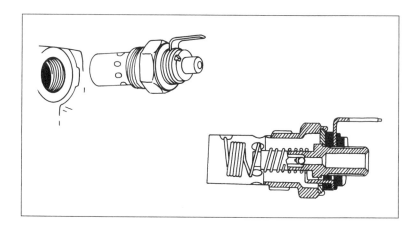

GLOW PLUGS

Glow plugs are electrically heated elements that heat the air/fuel mixture in the precombustion chamber. To test, operate the preheat switch:

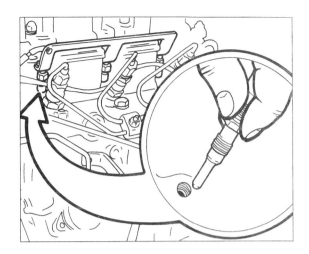

- The panel ammeter or dimming lights will indicate high current flow. Glow plugs can draw as much as 40 amps of current; or
- The glow plugs will feel warm.

Before replacing suspect glow plugs, check the voltage at the plug itself and make sure the relay is functioning. Corrosion on the glow-plug body can prevent good grounding. A multimeter set to measure resistance should indicate continuity through the plug element.

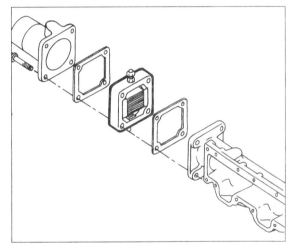

AIR HEATERS

Air heaters heat the air before it reaches the combustion chamber. Like glow plugs, they draw considerable current. The same tests as for glow plugs apply.

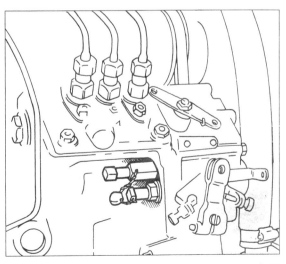

EXCESS-FUEL DEVICES

Excess-fuel devices are built into the injection pump or governor and provide extra fuel for starting—similar to a choke on a gasoline-engine carburetor. Excess-fuel devices are factory set and should not be adjusted.

FUEL INJECTORS

Although relatively simple in construction, fuel injectors are the most critical components in the diesel engine. They atomize fuel into the combustion chamber at temperatures above 1,000°C and pressures approaching 20,000 psi. They withstand constant vibration, yet still must operate as many as 10 times a second.

Small marine diesels use two main types of injector. Each injector has a specific spray pattern. The number, size, and angle of the jets is determined by the design of the engine.

Engines with swirl or pre-combustion chambers use injectors with pintle nozzles.

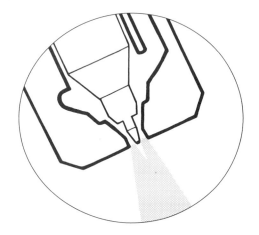

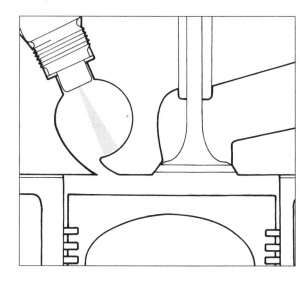

Direct-injection engines use injectors with multi-hole nozzles.

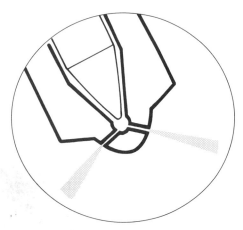

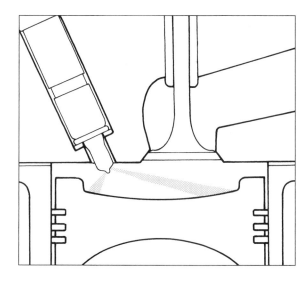

INJECTOR MAINTENANCE

Supplied with clean fuel, injectors require minimal maintenance and should give several thousand hours of reliable service. If nozzle holes and seats are worn, corroded, or contaminated, the injector will fail to atomize the fuel; raw fuel in the combustion chamber will not burn completely.

If your engine suffers from poor starting, loss of performance, erratic rpm, or excessive exhaust smoke, your problems are more likely due to defective injectors than to all the other causes combined.

Normal wear on injector nozzle seats can affect spray patterns as early as 1,000 hours. Severe wear or contamination will allow even more fuel to leak into the combustion chamber, causing damaging pre-ignition, or "knocking."

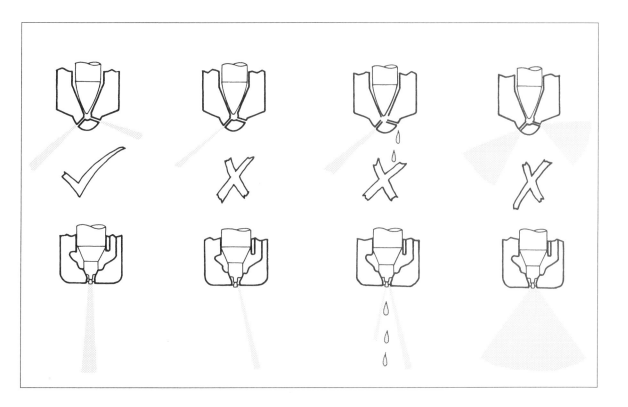

CHECKING OPERATION

The standard test to check a suspect injector is to run the engine at high idle and then momentarily loosen each injector supply line. No audible change in rpm identifies the problem injector. If an injector is causing knocking, the noise will disappear when its supply line is loosened. This test is very basic and

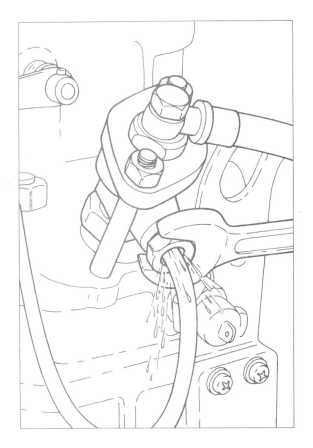
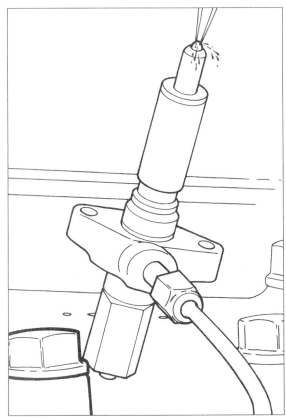

only confirms whether fuel is being delivered to the cylinder. It does not indicate whether the fuel is being correctly atomized.

A better test is to remove all injectors and reconnect them, inverted, to their supply lines. Turning the engine over with the starter will pump fuel through the injector; you can then examine the spray pattern. *Warning: Keep clear of atomized fuel. It is under high pressure and will penetrate skin and cause infection.*

If your injectors are defective, have them serviced by a qualified diesel shop.

REMOVING INJECTORS

Remove the supply and return fuel lines, taking care not to drop the sealing washers. If the injectors have not been regularly serviced, the combination of rust and carbon products can make them difficult to remove. If so, apply a good penetrating oil and rotate the injector side to side while lifting. For

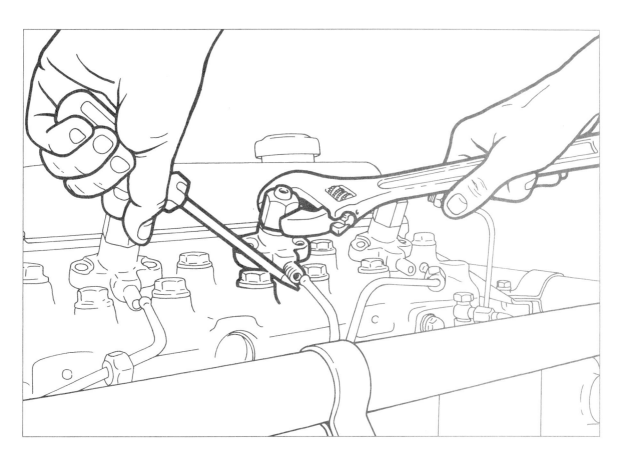

obstinate injectors, try loosening the retaining nuts slightly and using the cylinder's compression to eject them by turning the engine over on the starter.

REFITTING INJECTORS

Before refitting injectors, clean the injector holes of all carbon deposits. A wedge of paper towel jammed into the hole and turned with a large screwdriver is effective. To prevent leaks, replace all metal sealing washers—especially copper washers, which harden with age. In an emergency, you can soften copper washers by heating them to cherry red over the stove and then quenching them rapidly in water.

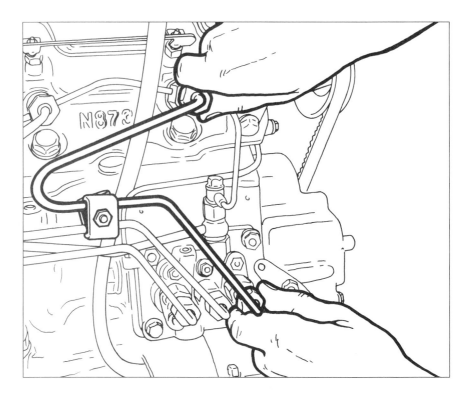

Take care not to pre-stress injector supply lines when refitting; this can lead to failure. You can correct a poor fit by removing the pipe completely and checking alignment at the injector pump and injector connections. If necessary, slightly bend the pipe to achieve a good fit before tightening the connections.

EMERGENCY REPAIRS

It is possible, in an emergency, to disassemble an injector for cleaning or even to replace a defective nozzle. Cleaning small nozzles, though, usually has only a temporary effect. If the injector uses shims for adjustment, the pressure setting should not drift too far when you reassemble the injector with the original parts. You can usually replace nozzles on injectors that use screw adjustment without disturbing the adjustment. Remember: Use this technique only in an emergency. It's better to carry a spare set of injectors aboard and have the problem injectors repaired at a diesel shop.

Carburetor cleaners will remove carbon and varnish buildup from nozzle valves; nevertheless, take great care to keep everything clean. These components are lapped to very smooth surfaces of close tolerance. Nozzle valves should slide easily.

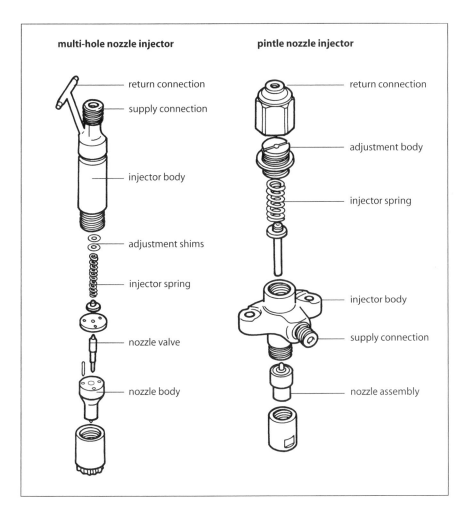

multi-hole nozzle injector

- return connection
- supply connection
- injector body
- adjustment shims
- injector spring
- nozzle valve
- nozzle body

pintle nozzle injector

- return connection
- adjustment body
- injector spring
- injector body
- supply connection
- nozzle assembly

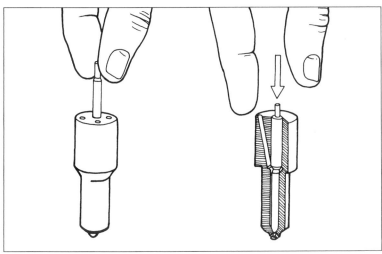

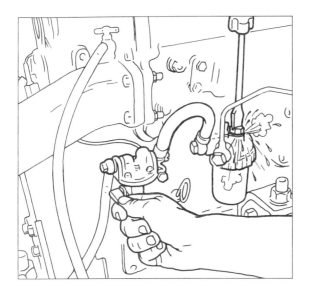

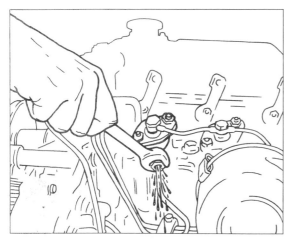

AIR IN THE FUEL SYSTEM

Air can find its way into the fuel system by several routes. It is normally sucked into the fuel supply through a poor seal upstream of the lift pump. Downstream of the lift pump the system is pressurized, and a faulty seal will result in an external fuel leak when the engine is running. *The most common cause of air in the fuel system is insufficient bleeding after a fuel-filter change.*

BLEEDING AIR FROM THE FUEL SYSTEM

Bleed the system in the following sequence:

1. Loosen the bleed screw at the top of the secondary filter. Operate the external lever on the fuel-lift pump. If the lever is only pumping at the bottom of the stroke, rotate the crankshaft one full turn to reposition the cam lobe. Continue pumping until air-free fuel flows from the screw, then tighten the bleed screw. If the primary-filter element has just been changed, it may take some time to clear all the air. If air remains, check the primary-filter seals and lift pump.

2. Loosen the bleed screw on the injector pump and continue operating the lift pump until the fuel is free of air. If the pump has more than one bleed screw, bleed the lower one first. Tighten the bleed screw(s).

3. Loosen all the injector supply lines at the injector. Turn the engine over with the starter until air-free fuel flows in spurts from each line. Retighten.

FUEL SYSTEM FAULTS

Problem	Possible Cause	Possible Symptoms
FUEL CONTAMINATION		
Water	Source suspect [1] Deck-plate filler leaking [3] Condensation [3]	White smoke; difficult starting; loss of power
Air	Poor sealing on primary filter [1] Leaking pipes, hoses, and connections [2] Fuel valves shut off [3] Lift pump defective [3] No fuel in tank [4] Tank pickup tube defective [5]	Difficult starting; erratic rpm; engine dies
Algae or fungus growth	Water in fuel [2]	Primary filter or fuel lines clogged with black, stringy debris; difficult starting; erratic rpm; engine dies
Incorrect grade	Source suspect [5]	Difficult starting; loss of power; black smoke
FUEL FILTERS		
Air in fuel	Defective sealing [1] Leaking pipes between tank and filter [3]	Difficult starting; erratic rpm; engine dies
Clogged	Filter not changed often enough [1] Tank dirty [3]	As above
LIFT PUMP		
Not pumping	Internal valves contaminated or broken [3] External non-return valve, if fitted, stuck closed [3] Diaphragm leaking [4]	As above Fuel in oil sump; engine appears to be "making oil"
INJECTOR PUMP		
Not pumping	Air in fuel system [1] Lift pump defective [3] Filters clogged [3] Injector pump defective [4]	Engine will not run; difficult starting; rough running; erratic rpm; engine dies

INJECTOR LINES

Problem	Possible Cause	Possible Symptoms
Cracked	Vibration [3] Inadequate pipe support [3] Pre-stressed on installation [3]	External fuel leaks; rough running; vibration; loss of power
Not sealing	Nut loose [2] Conical sealing surfaces damaged [2]	As above

INJECTORS

Problem	Possible Cause	Possible Symptoms
Nozzle stuck open	Contamination [2] Wear [2]	Knocking (pre-ignition); loss of power; white smoke; black smoke
Nozzle stuck closed	Contamination [2] Wear [2]	Uneven injection; rough running; loss of power; vibration; difficult starting
Nozzle eroded	Wear [2] Water in fuel [2]	Knocking (pre-ignition); loss of power; white smoke; difficult starting
Pressure high	Incorrect setting [3]	Difficult starting
Pressure low	Wear [2] Incorrect setting [3]	Difficult starting; white smoke; loss of power
Spring broken	Fatigue [5]	Difficult starting; low power; rough running
Two sealing washers under injector	Poor maintenance [3]	Black smoke; difficult starting

GOVERNOR

Problem	Possible Cause	Possible Symptoms
Sticking	Wear [4] Contamination [3]	Loss of power; erratic rpm
Weights defective	Governor components loose [5]	Low maximum rpm
Spring defective	Fatigue [4] Governor components loose [4]	High rpm; erratic rpm

COLD-STARTING AID

Problem	Possible Cause	Possible Symptoms
Not functioning	No electrical supply [2] No fuel supply [3] Poor grounding [3] Defective [3]	Difficult starting

Problem	Possible Cause	Possible Symptoms
TIMING		
Advanced	Injector pump loose [3] Set incorrectly [4] Governor sticking [4]	Knocking; rough idle; difficult starting; black smoke
Retarded	As above	Loss of power; overheating; white smoke

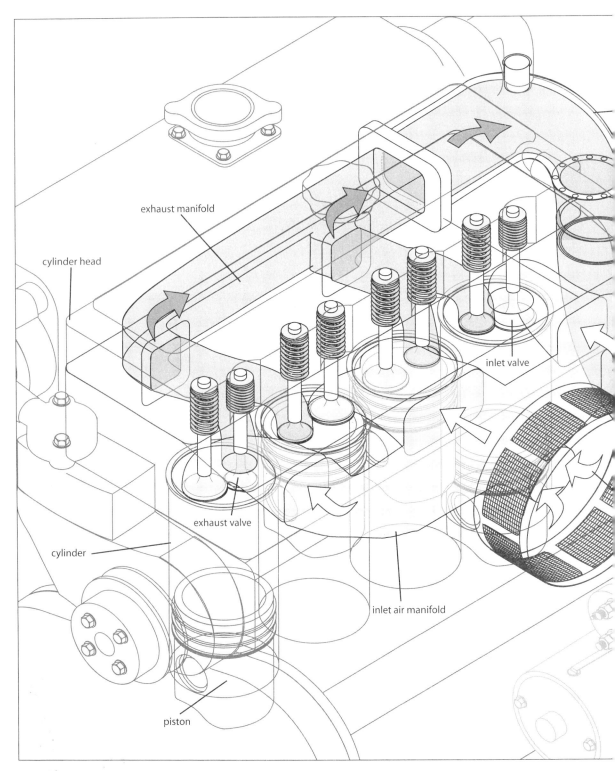

exhaust manifold

cylinder head

inlet valve

exhaust valve

cylinder

inlet air manifold

piston

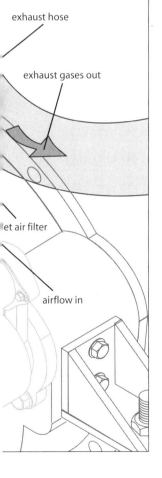

exhaust injection
elbow

exhaust hose

exhaust gases out

et air filter

airflow in

8

THE INTAKE
AND EXHAUST SYSTEM

A small four-cylinder engine running at high speed will typically consume more than 6,000 cubic feet of air per hour. Not all of it is necessary for combustion, but restrict the air flow and the burn will be incomplete, producing more carbon monoxide and black soot.

It is therefore critical that air flows unrestricted through the intake and exhaust system. Engine rooms must be well ventilated, and exhaust systems well designed.

The more air in the cylinders, the more fuel can be burned, which in turn means more power. With a trend toward small, light, high-power diesels, turbocharging offers an effective method of increasing the amount of air that can be packed into the cylinders, boosting output by as much as 50%.

Larger engines are often fitted with an intake-air cooler, or intercooler, to lower the air temperature. This increases the density of air, so even more can be packed into the cylinders.

The exhaust system not only removes harmful gases, it also carries away 50% of the engine's excess heat. In small marine engines, raw water is injected into the exhaust system to reduce the temperature of gases and hot exhaust pipes. Wet-exhaust systems operate at sufficiently low temperatures to allow the use of flexible-rubber exhaust hose and fiberglass mufflers.

Intake and exhaust systems require minimal maintenance. Periodic air-filter cleaning and a visual inspection will usually locate potential problems.

A badly designed exhaust system can restrict gas flow, which will cause difficult starting, loss of power, and premature engine wear. Correct muffler sizing and hose routing will prevent raw water from flowing back into the cylinders and destroying the engine.

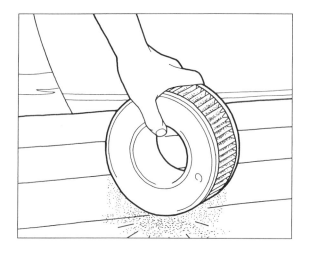

AIR-INTAKE FILTER

The minimal dust and dirt in an engine compartment means marine air filters need not work quite as hard as their automotive counterparts. Still, an air-intake filter stops dirt from entering the engine and scoring the cylinder bores, and so improves oil consumption and extends engine life. A well-designed filter assembly can also reduce engine noise.

In many engines, coarse metal or plastic screens on the intake manifold stop larger debris from being sucked into the engine. Paper or foam elements improve filtration further, but require more frequent servicing to maintain good airflow. Water- or oil-soaked elements restrict airflow severely. Excessive oil on the filter or inside the intake manifold suggests that worn cylinders and/or piston rings are causing high crankcase pressure.

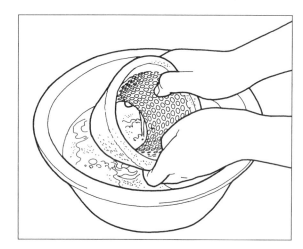

SERVICING FILTER ELEMENTS

Although maintenance is relatively simple, owners tend to ignore air filters and seldom service them properly.

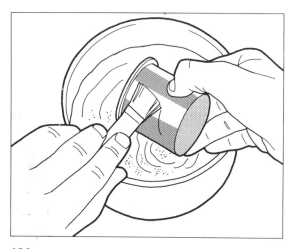

- Tap paper elements on a flat surface to dislodge loose dirt particles. It's impossible to successfully wash paper elements. If the contamination is heavy or oily, they should be replaced.
- Wash foam elements with a mild detergent solution. Dry the element before refitting.
- Wash metal elements in solvent.

EXHAUST MANIFOLD

For the most part, exhaust manifolds are water cooled. Chapter 6 covers fresh-water– or coolant-cooled exhaust manifolds that incorporate the header tank and heat exchanger. Raw-water–cooled exhaust manifolds are prone to internal corrosion. Periodically remove hoses and covers to inspect for restricted waterways. The same instructions apply as for cleaning the exhaust injection elbow, covered below.

EXHAUST INJECTION ELBOW

The exhaust injection elbow is the point at which cooling raw water is injected into the exhaust system to cool and silence the exhaust gases. Injection elbows come in all shapes and sizes and may be made of aluminum, cast iron, steel, stainless, and even bronze. Because no metal is totally resistant to the corrosive effects of sea water and hot exhaust gases, injection elbows have a heavy wall thickness.

INSPECTION

Salt or corrosion products indicate a leak caused by severe corrosion. The first indication usually is small, pin-prick–sized holes opposite the point where raw water is injected into the elbow. Soot deposits by the mounting flange indicate a loose joint or gasket failure. Check the tightness of attachment bolts, which loosen due to high temperatures and the settling of thick gaskets.

Exhaust injection elbows restrict easily with buildup of oily carbon and corrosion deposits, especially if the engine is run at low rpm for long periods to charge batteries. The elbow should be inspected internally every other

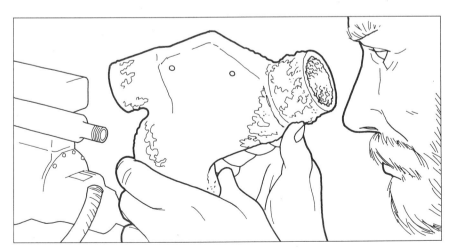

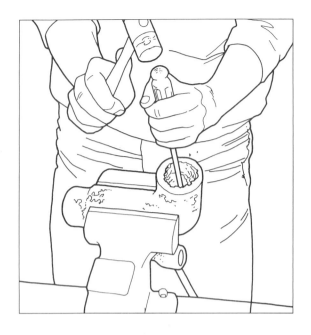

season. However, removal can be one of those tasks that's easier said than done, especially with stiff wire-reinforced exhaust hose, corrosion, and limited access!

CLEANING

The most effective cleaning method is sandblasting, but not everyone has access to this equipment. Dipping in acid is risky: It can eat too much base metal. Carburetor-choke cleaners are reasonably effective at removing soot deposits but work slowly. You can also chip with a hammer and screwdriver, but this can be time consuming.

Corrosion attacks elbows of cast iron more than those made of other metals—particularly if the engine runs infrequently. Thick flakes of iron will break off during chipping. If you're working on an older diesel, have a replacement handy before attacking severe corrosion.

EXHAUST HOSE

Because wet-exhaust systems run at relatively low temperatures, they pose little fire risk aboard a boat. Lower exhaust temperatures also mean that you can run lighter fiberglass tubing and flexible piping materials such as wire-reinforced rubber hose. Do not use plastic tubing: It increases the risk of fire if the raw-water supply is disrupted.

INSPECTION

Almost every small marine diesel exhaust system uses rubber hose reinforced with spiral-wound steel wire. The hose is maintenance free, but deteriorates with age; inspect it every 12 months for kinking, cracking, corroded wire, and delamination.

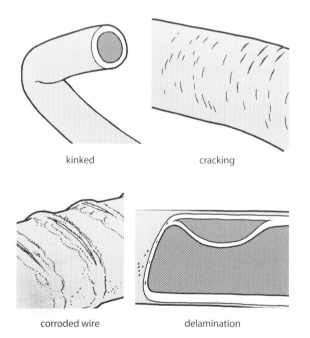

kinked   cracking

corroded wire   delamination

MUFFLERS AND LIFT BOXES

Wet-exhaust lift mufflers use exhaust pressure to lift pellets of raw water through the exhaust hose and overboard. A good installation requires only seasonal inspection, but a bad one can cause high exhaust backpressure or allow water to flow back into the cylinder head and destroy the engine. Questionable installations should be inspected by a professional.

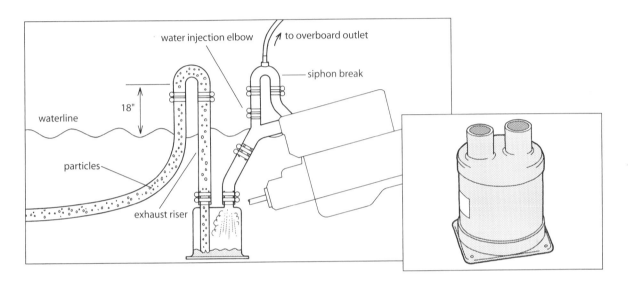

EXHAUST BACKPRESSURE

An unrestricted path for exhaust gases is equally important as a good supply of intake air. Resistance within the exhaust system will result in high backpressure, causing difficult starting, loss of power, and increased engine wear.

MEASURING BACKPRESSURE

Backpressure can be measured with a sensitive 0–5 psi gauge attached to a football inflator nozzle. Make a small hole in the exhaust hose close to the injection elbow with a sharp spike, and insert the nozzle. Take readings with the engine running at maximum rpm. Pressures on wet exhaust systems fluctuate as the lift box expels a pellet of water; take an average reading. As a general rule, backpressure should not exceed 2.0 psi (52 inches of water) on naturally aspirated engines, or 1.25 psi (32 inches of water) on turbocharged engines. Many manufacturers specify even lower limits.

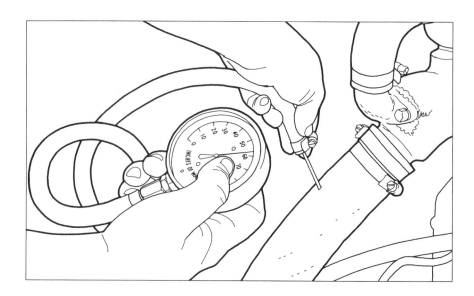

REDUCING BACKPRESSURE

Exhaust-hose diameter. Never reduce the hose below the size of the injection elbow.

Hose length. Minimize the length of exhaust hose. If the transom is far from the engine, exit through the side of the hull.

Hose routing. Raise the hose as high as possible immediately after the muffler to keep out following seas. The hose should drop gradually toward the outlet, with no dips to collect water.

Bends and elbows. Minimize elbows and sharp bends in the hose.

Lift box. The lift box must be of adequate size. Its volume should be at least twice (ideally, three times) the volume of the hose to the top of the first loop.

Exhaust through-hull. The through-hull must match the exhaust-hose size, and should offer no restrictions.

TURBOCHARGERS

Turbochargers increase an engine's output by harnessing the normally wasted energy from hot exhaust gases to pack more air into the cylinders.

Turbochargers are surprisingly reliable—especially when you consider that some of the smaller units spin at almost 200,000 rpm. There is little an amateur mechanic can do to service this high-speed air pump other than to inspect it regularly and clean the compressor. Replace a defective turbocharger.

INSPECTION

- Remove the air filter and check the compressor wheel for cleanliness. Excessive oil suggests seal failure. Wash the compressor if dirty (see below).
- Spin the shaft slowly by hand and check that there is no contact between either wheel and the housings.
- The bearings should feel smooth, with minimal shaft end float or radial play.

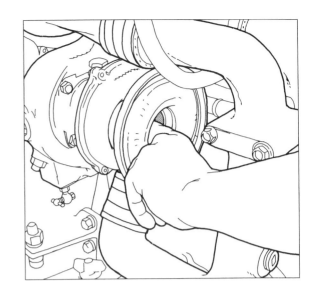

WASHING

Keep turbocharger compressor blades clean to maintain efficient airflow. Compressors can quickly become contaminated with an oil film that collects dirt and dust. Engine manufacturers specify how often to wash compressors, but intervals between cleanings depend on the cleanliness of the air in the engine room. To wash the compressor, run the engine up to high rpm and spray the manufacturer's recommended cleaning solution into the intake.

INTERCOOLERS

Intercoolers should be maintenance free; nevertheless, you should remove them periodically to clean and inspect. The small gaps between intercooler fins tend to collect dirt, especially if there is oil in the intake.

Pressure-test the unit if you find any corrosion. Remember: Most intercoolers use raw water to cool the intake air, so an internal failure can allow raw water to enter the cylinders and destroy the engine.

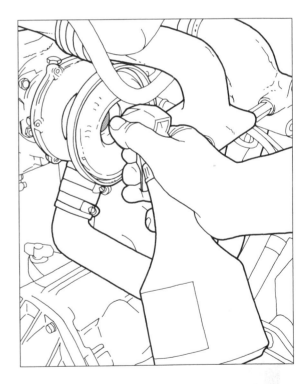

INTAKE AND EXHAUST SYSTEM FAULTS

Problem	Possible Cause	Possible Symptoms

INTAKE FILTER

Contaminated	Excessive oil from crankcase breather [2] Element wet [2] Environment dirty or dusty [4]	Loss of power; black/dark smoke; low maximum rpm

EXCESSIVE SMOKE—See Troubleshooting Chart 7, page 36

White smoke—water in fuel	Contaminated fuel [2] Defective cylinder-head gasket [3]	Misfiring; loss of power; poor starting
White smoke—unburned fuel	Defective injector [1] Insufficient compression [3] Low air temperature [3] Incorrect timing [4] Incorrect fuel grade [5]	As above
Blue smoke—burned oil	Oil overfilled [2] Worn valve guides [3] Worn piston rings/cylinders [3] Incorrect fuel grade [5]	High oil consumption
Black/dark smoke—partially burned fuel	Engine overloaded [2] Blocked air filter [2] Defective injectors [3] Incorrect timing [4]	Loss of power

HIGH BACKPRESSURE

	Poor design [1] Buildup of carbon at exhaust injection elbow [2] Collapsed exhaust hose [3]	Loss of power; poor starting; engine dies; low maximum rpm

EXHAUST TEMPERATURE HIGH

	Insufficient raw-water cooling [2] Engine overloaded [3]	Steam from exhaust; exhaust hose hot to touch

EXHAUST INJECTION ELBOW

Restricted	Excessive periods at idle [2] Corrosion [2] Oil contamination [3]	White/blue smoke; difficult starting; loss of power; low maximum rpm

TURBOCHARGER

Inefficient	Dirty compressor [2] Seized [3]	Reduced performance; dark exhaust smoke
Noisy	Bearings worn [3] Damaged compressor or turbine blades [3]	As above
Water leaks	Loose manifold nuts [3] Defective gasket [3] Corrosion [4]	Water in cylinder head; engine seized; external corrosion salts
Oil leaks	Worn or damaged seals [3] Oil drain blocked [3]	Blue exhaust smoke; high oil consumption

INTERCOOLER

Water leaks	Corrosion [3] Gasket failure [3]	Water in cylinder head; seized engine
Air leaks	Loose joints [2] Corrosion [3] Gasket failure [3]	Loss of performance

EXHAUST HOSE

Delaminating	Deterioration of bonding between layers, often due to excessive oil and fuel contact
Soft	External deterioration due to prolonged contact with fuel and oil, often from sitting in an oil-filled bilge
Rusting	Internal wire corrosion; water will seep along wire and destroy reinforcing, which will promote delamination
Kinked	Bends too sharp
Cracking	External rubber cracks with age

HOW LIKELY?   [1] Very common   [2] Common   [3] Possible   [4] Rare   [5] Very rare

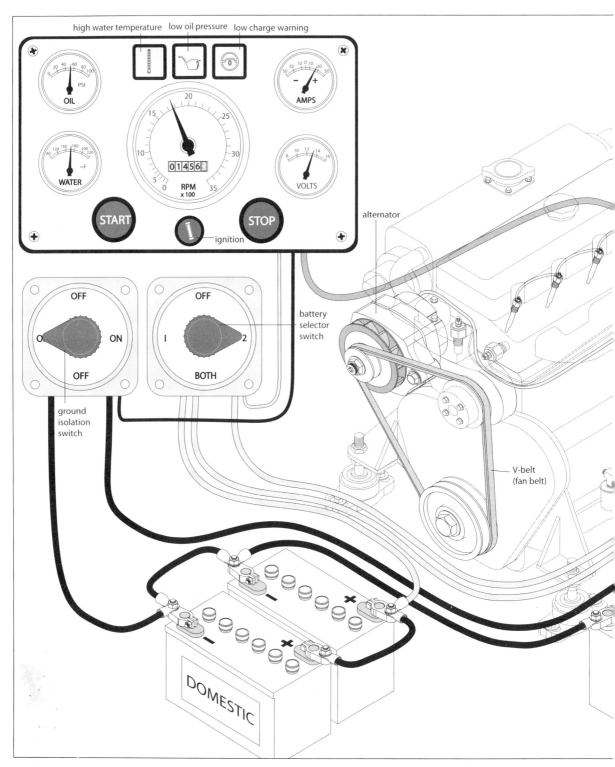

high water temperature   low oil pressure   low charge warning

OIL
PSI
20 40 60 80 100
0

WATER
120 160 180 200 220
80   ∞F

AMPS
50 30 10 0 10 30 50
−   +

VOLTS
8   10 12 14 16

RPM
x 100
20
15   25
10   30
5   35
0
01456

START   STOP

ignition

alternator

OFF
ON
OFF

OFF
1   2
BOTH

battery
selector
switch

ground
isolation
switch

V-belt
(fan belt)

DOMESTIC

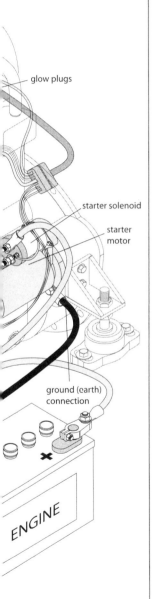

glow plugs

starter solenoid

starter motor

ground (earth) connection

ENGINE

9

THE ELECTRICAL SYSTEM

The typical sailboat diesel has two electrical circuits: one for engine starting, and one for charging. The starting circuit consists of a battery, a starter motor, and the wiring and switches to connect the two.

Starters themselves are generally reliable, unless they are overheated or soaked with water from the bilge or leaking wet-exhaust connections.

Starting-circuit problems are common, and usually due to low battery output or poor connections. Check these connections regularly for tightness and corrosion; in other respects, the starting circuit will look after itself.

The main component in the charging circuit is the alternator, which charges the battery banks and supplies power for the boat's electrical equipment.

Most faults with the charging circuit are caused by the alternator failing to charge the batteries, or overcharging caused by a defective or incorrectly modified voltage regulator.

Routine maintenance for the charging circuit involves monitoring the batteries and the V-belt that drives the alternator.

It is not within the scope of this book to cover wiring in detail, but whenever you inspect your engine, pay particular attention to the wiring. Wire must be correctly sized. The high resistance of a wire too small for the current it has to carry will create considerable heat that can lead to fire.

BATTERIES

There are three types of batteries used in marine applications: wet lead-acid, gel lead-acid, and occasionally, nickel-cadmium. Although the wet lead-acid type requires more maintenance than the other two, it is generally a better value for the money and by far the most popular.

Batteries come in all shapes and sizes. The standard internal configuration is six cells, each generating just over 2 volts. Batteries can be connected in parallel to increase capacity, or in series to increase voltage. Six-volt and 8-volt batteries are commonly combined to make up banks of 12, 24, and 32 volts.

WHICH BATTERY?

Engine-starting batteries must deliver high amperage in short bursts. The starter on a four-cylinder auxiliary diesel will typically draw more than 350 amps during start. Dedicated starting batteries should be the cranking type, designed with thinner, often porous, plates for rapid discharge; they must be large enough to provide adequate cranking power—especially for cold starting.

Although you must consider weight and size, it's better to have spare capacity than not enough. As a general rule, the battery should provide 2 to 3 cranking amps for each engine cubic inch. A 2-liter diesel, for example, would need at a minimum a battery capable of about 250 cranking amps.

The house, or domestic, batteries must be capable of handling all the

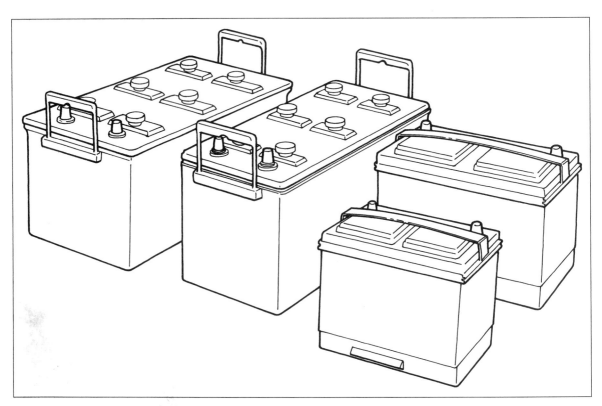

remaining demands of a boat's electrical system. House batteries should be of the deep-cycle type, which have thicker plates and separators to better handle deep discharge. Six-volt, deep-cycle golf-cart batteries are proving very successful in marine applications, exhibiting excellent capacity and long life. Deep-cycle batteries can be used as starting batteries, provided they are large enough to recover from high discharge rates.

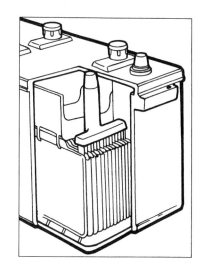

TESTING

To test a battery's charge level, measure the specific gravity of each cell's electrolyte with a hydrometer. A fully charged cell should read above 1.260 SG; adjust your readings for temperature according to the scale on the hydrometer.

% CHARGED	SPECIFIC GRAVITY	VOLTAGE
100%	1.265–1.275	12.6
75%	1.225–1.235	12.4
50%	1.190–1.200	12.2
25%	1.155–1.165	12.0
0%	1.120–1.130	11.7

Load testing is also an effective method of checking a battery's

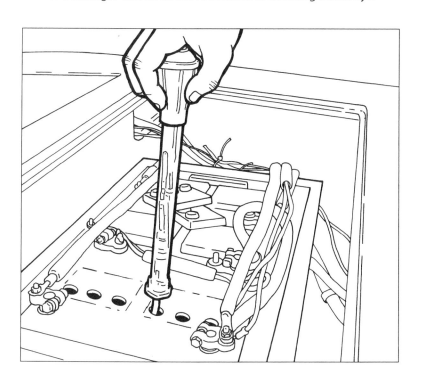

condition. Although commercial testers are available, measuring the voltage of the
battery during the start cycle will produce similar results. To conduct the test, charge the battery fully and pull the stop cable so the engine won't start. Voltage must remain above 80% of the no-load voltage; a typical 12-volt battery, for example, must not drop below 9.5 volts. If the battery fails this test, replace it: It is either defective or too small for the job.

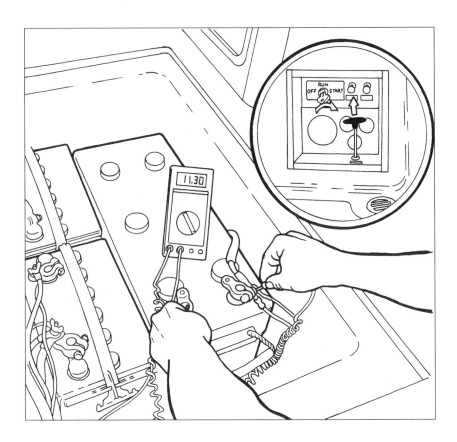

CHARGING

Battery-charging requires carefully controlled voltage. Alternator voltage regulators, which sense battery voltage and adjust alternator output accordingly, are usually preset between 14.2 and 14.4 volts. Above 13.8 volts, the electrolyte starts to gas and the water in the electrolyte begins to evaporate. Higher voltages cause the electrolyte to boil, and the cells will need constant filling. The heat of severe overcharging distorts the plates and will eventually destroy the battery. Do not charge gel cells over 14.1 volts.

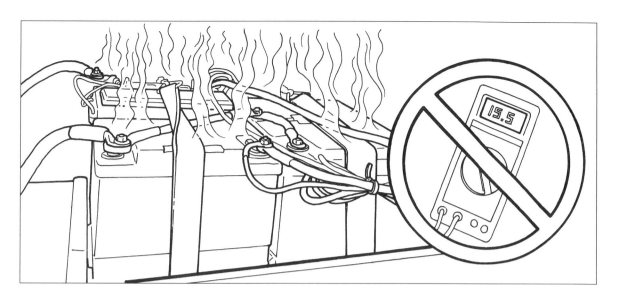

MAINTENANCE

Batteries don't like being deeply discharged; if left in that state for a period of time, capacity-reducing lead sulfate forms on the plates and can be difficult to remove. Keep the battery well charged, avoid discharging it below 50%, and maintain the correct electrolyte levels to ensure maximum life. Top off wet cells with distilled water; drinking water is acceptable, provided it is not high in mineral salts.

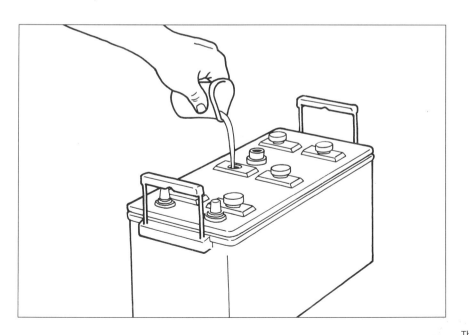

BATTERY SWITCHES

Battery switches select individual batteries, connect multiple batteries in parallel, and allow the batteries to be disconnected in an emergency or when not in use. Battery switches must be of adequate size for the current they conduct. Check occasionally for loose connections, and regularly apply a light spray of corrosion inhibitor.

Warning: Never disconnect batteries while the engine is running: It will cause a voltage surge in the alternator that can damage diodes and transistorized regulators.

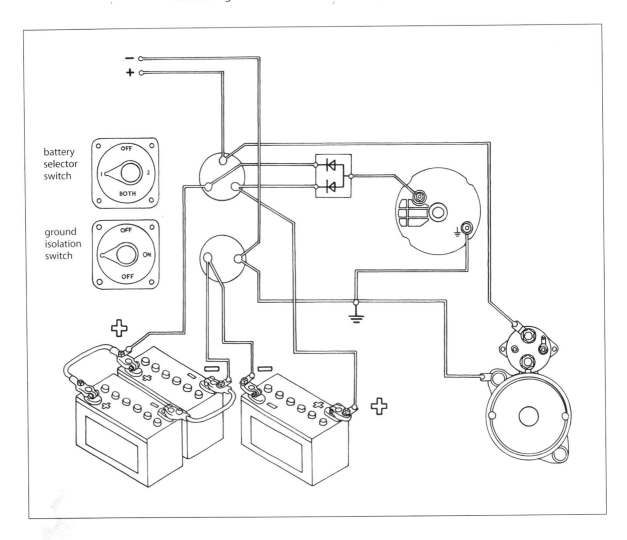

ALTERNATOR

An alternator operated without modification can last almost the life of the engine without maintenance.

INSPECTION

With the V-belt removed, an alternator should make little noise when spun by hand. There should be no contact between the rotor and the stator coils, the fan shouldn't rub, and the bearings should feel smooth. The alternator pulley width must match with the crankshaft and circulating pump pulleys and be correctly aligned. Refer to Chapter 6 for information on tensioning the V-belt.

TESTING

Check the output shown on the panel ammeter, if fitted. Measure output voltage with a voltmeter, touching one probe to the + output terminal and the other to the casing ground. Any reading above battery voltage indicates some level of charging. With a low battery, expect the voltage to be close to 13.0V, rising to 14.2V as the battery reaches full charge.

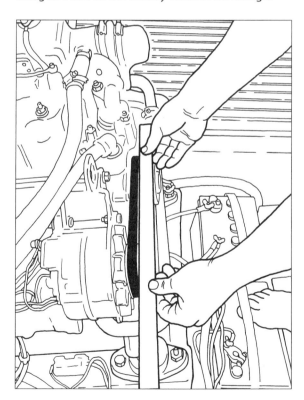

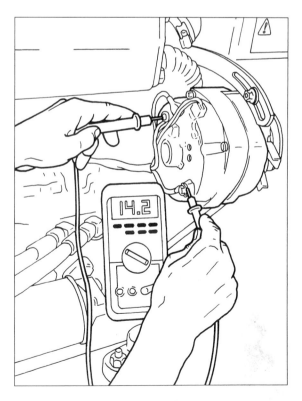

MAINTENANCE

Although testing and replacing internal regulators, rectifiers, and brushes is not particularly difficult, variations in alternator design make it impractical to adequately cover this topic here. Reconditioned alternators are inexpensive; carry a spare on board.

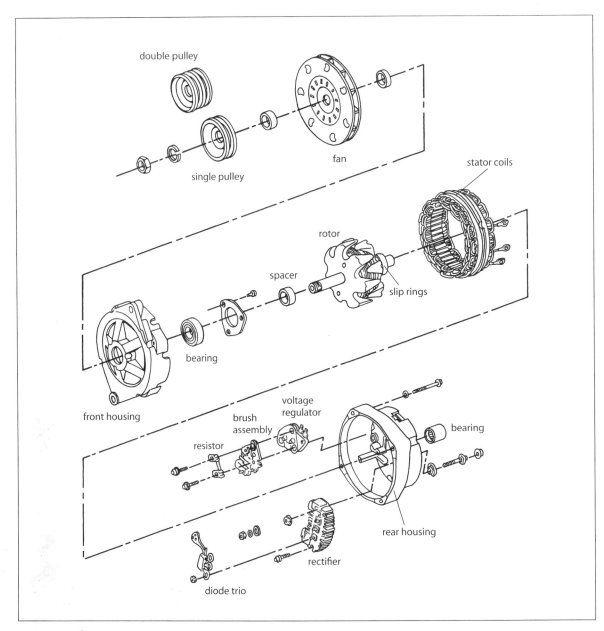

double pulley

single pulley

fan

stator coils

rotor

spacer

slip rings

bearing

front housing

voltage regulator

brush assembly

resistor

bearing

rear housing

rectifier

diode trio

IMPROVING OUTPUT

Standard marine-engine alternators use automotive-type voltage regulators that allow charging at a relatively low rate after an initial high charge. This is fine for a vessel whose engine runs constantly, but a sailboat would have to idle its engine for hours every day to keep up with normal domestic electrical needs. Many owners replace the standard alternator with higher-output units whose computerized, step-charging regulators charge the batteries more efficiently. If you upgrade your alternator, be sure the pulley matches those on the crankshaft and circulating pump and that the V-belt can handle the job.

You can easily and cheaply increase the output of a standard alternator by reducing the voltage the regulator senses. Insert a diode of adequate size (IN5400 or larger) into the sensing circuit. It is not the diode's one-way flow that's important in this instance, but the nominal ¾-volt drop across the diode. This fools the voltage regulator into "thinking" that the battery voltage is lower than it really is, and the regulator increases the charge rate accordingly.

Use a switch to route the sensing circuit through the diode, and you will have the option of a high or low charge rate. More than a single diode in the circuit will further increase the charge rate, but you may burn out the alternator or overcharge the batteries.

This modification should also be applied to alternators that charge batteries through isolation diodes to compensate for the voltage drop.

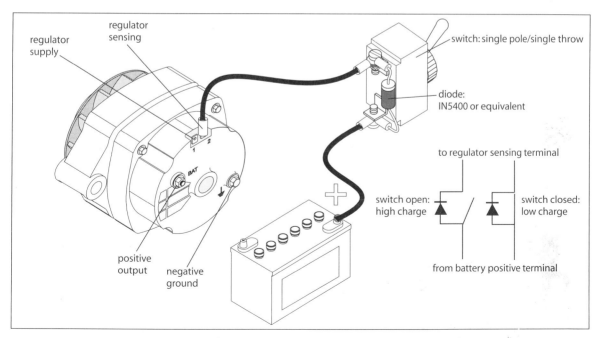

STARTER MOTOR

Starter motors are generally of two types. Pre-engaged starters use an external solenoid to engage the drive gear with the flywheel ring gear before the motor itself is energized. Inertia starters use centrifugal force on a helical slot to throw the drive gear into the flywheel when the motor is energized. This mechanism is commonly called a Bendix. Solenoids on inertia starters just switch the high current.

TESTING

Most starter problems are with the supply voltage rather than the starter motor. Voltage measured at the starter terminals during the start cycle should be higher than 80% of the battery voltage—more than 9.5 volts for a 12-volt system. Starters that pass this test but still fail to turn the engine over enough to start the engine either have a bad ground or are defective.

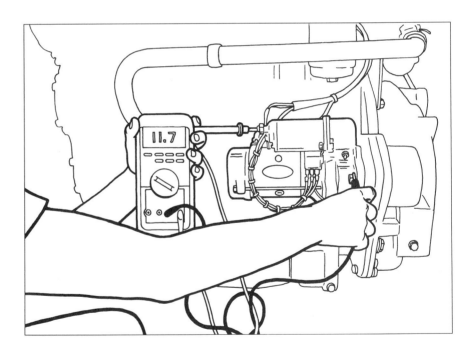

MAINTENANCE

Starters are generally maintenance free and should give years of service if kept clean, dry, and free of corrosion. Solenoids on pre-engaged starters tend to stick. You can replace these solenoids, as they're generally sold separately.

Inertia starters are prone to corrosion, dirt, or wear to the Bendix mechanism that prevents the gear from engaging. You can often solve the problem by removing the starter and cleaning and greasing the Bendix.

TYPICAL ENGINE-INSTALLATION CIRCUIT DIAGRAM

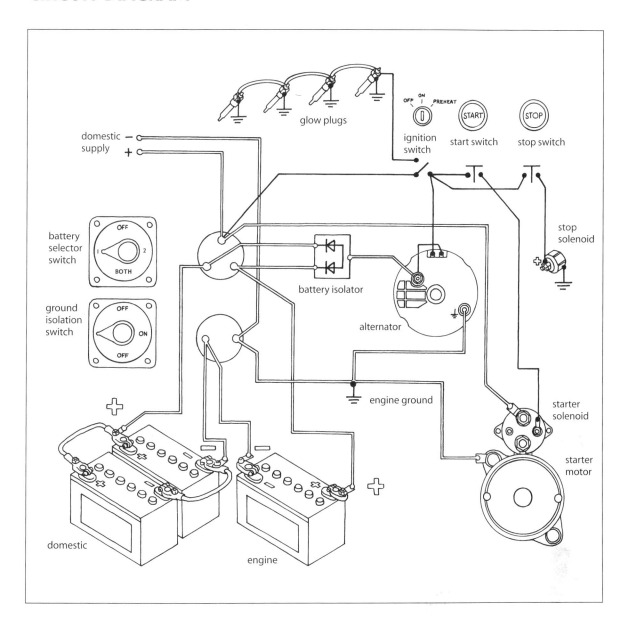

ELECTRICAL SYSTEM FAULTS

Problem	Possible Cause	Possible Symptoms

STARTING SYSTEM PROBLEMS—See Troubleshooting Chart 8, page 38

CHARGING SYSTEM PROBLEMS—See Troubleshooting Chart 9, page 40

START SWITCH

Open circuit	Defective switch [3] Loose terminals [3] Corroded terminals [3]	Starter fails to operate; no voltage at starter solenoid positive terminal when selected
Short circuit	Defective switch—mechanically jammed in selected position [3] Water contamination [3]	Starter engages as soon as battery isolator is switched on

STARTER MOTOR

Brushes worn	Normal wear [3] Commutator scored [3]	Starter fails to operate or turns slowly
Internal short circuit	Contaminated with water [2] Wiring chafed [3]	Starter fails to operate or turns slowly; starter draws high current when selected
Internal open circuit	Corrosion [3] Loose or broken wiring [4]	Starter fails to operate or has reduced power; starter draws low current when selected
Internal contamination	Water ingress from exhaust manifold or heat exchanger [3] Oil from defective flywheel oil seal [3] Water from bottom of flywheel sitting in high bilgewater [3]	As above
Drive gear defective	Bendix defective (inertia starters only) [2] Clutch mechanism jammed or broken [3]	Starter overspeeds and fails to turn the engine over

Problem	Possible Cause	Possible Symptoms

STARTER SOLENOID—Pre-Engaged Starters

Problem	Possible Cause	Possible Symptoms
Jammed in "off" position	Contamination [3] Wear [3]	Starter will not operate
Jammed in "on" position	Contamination [3] Wear [3]	Starter runs continuously, even when start switch is released; starter may overspeed
Corroded or eroded contacts	Normal wear [2] Contacts wet at some time [3]	Starter intermittent or slow-turning

BATTERY

Problem	Possible Cause	Possible Symptoms
Low output	Discharged [1] Low electrolyte [1] Sulfated [2] Distorted plates [2] Loose terminals [2] Corroded terminals [2]	Starter fails to operate; starter turns engine over slowly; starter solenoid only clicks; lights dim excessively when start selected
Will not hold charge	Low electrolyte [1] Sulfated [2] Distorted plates [2]	As above

ALTERNATOR

Problem	Possible Cause	Possible Symptoms
Overcharging	Voltage regulator defective [2] Battery sensing wire disconnected [3]	Electrolyte boils; smells of acid
Not charging	V-belt broken or slipping [2] Voltage regulator defective [2] Brushes worn or contaminated [3]	No increase in voltage when engine starts; charge light stays on
Undercharging	Inadequate charging time [1] V-belt slipping [2] Battery defective [2] Corroded or loose terminals [2]	Battery never reaches full charge

HOW LIKELY? [1] Very common   [2] Common   [3] Possible   [4] Rare   [5] Very rare

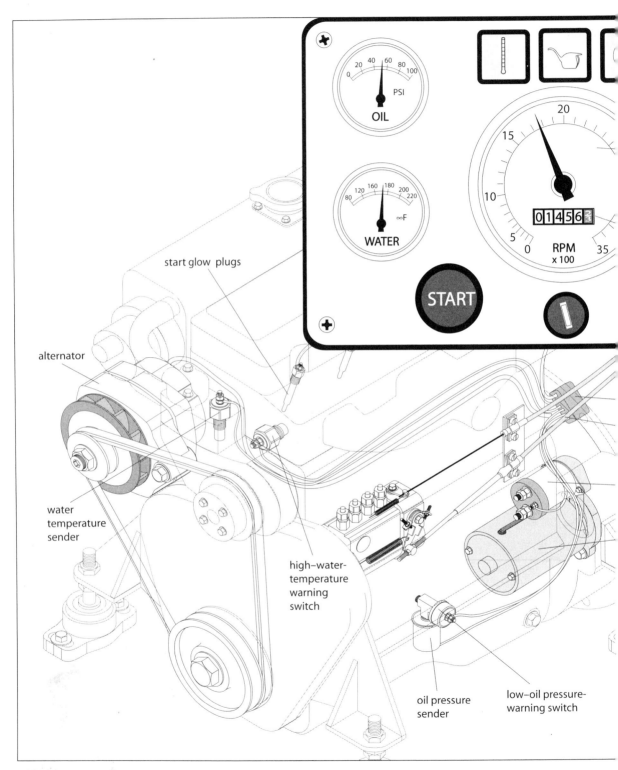

OIL

PSI

20 40 60 80
0 100

WATER

°F

120 160 180 200
80 220

20

15

10

5
0

RPM
x 100

35

01456

START

start glow plugs

alternator

water
temperature
sender

high–water-
temperature
warning
switch

oil pressure
sender

low–oil pressure-
warning switch

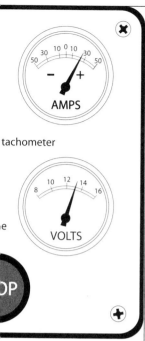

tachometer

VOLTS

shutdown cable

gine wiring loom connector

rottle (accelerator cable)

— starter solenoid

— starter motor

10
CONTROLS AND INSTRUMENTS

Whether attached to the binnacle or to the side of the cockpit, start, stop, throttle, and gear-selector controls should be within easy reach of the helmsman. These cable-operated remote controls usually are reliable and require little maintenance.

It's best to place instruments and warning lights in a visible location, sheltered from the elements. Every instrument panel should include a tachometer and warning lights connected to alarm circuits for low oil pressure and high coolant temperature. Oil-pressure and water-temperature gauges allow the helmsman to continuously monitor the condition of these two important systems.

THROTTLE CONTROLS

Engine idle and maximum rpm are set by stops on the governor or injector pump (see Chapter 7). The throttle lever must allow unrestricted movement between these stops.

CHECKING TRAVEL

To check the throttle controls, disconnect the end fitting from the throttle arm on the engine. Pull the control lever all the way back, and make sure the end fitting travels beyond the idle stop. With the engine arm against the maximum stop, push the control lever all the way forward and make sure the connector travels beyond its mounting hole. If it passes these two tests, reconnect the end fitting.

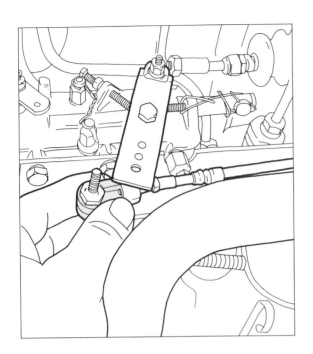

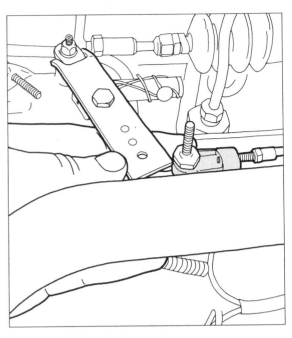

ADJUSTMENTS

To increase or decrease the amount of cable travel, move the end fitting into a lever-arm hole farther from or closer to the pivot. To bias the travel toward the idle or maximum stops, adjust the position of the end fitting on the cable, and remember to tighten the locknut or clamp screw when finished.

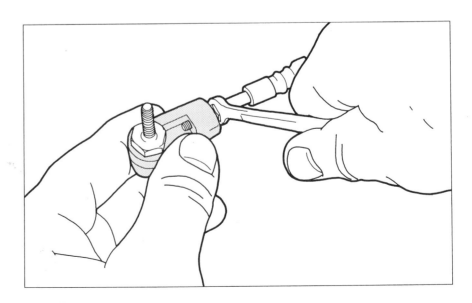

GEAR-SELECTOR CONTROLS

The gear-selector control doesn't have stops to define the limit of travel. You must, however, move the gearbox-selection lever fully into gear; partial selection is a major cause of gearbox failure.

CHECKING TRAVEL

Place the shift lever in neutral and disconnect the cable end fitting at the gearbox lever. The cable must approach the lever at a 90° angle.

Push the shift lever into the forward position and check that the cable end fitting at the gearbox travels beyond the position where the gearbox lever makes positive forward selection. Do the same test for reverse.

ADJUSTMENTS

If the cable does not approach the gear-selector lever at a 90° angle in neutral, reposition the clamp that holds the cable jacket. This setting must be correct before you make other adjustments. To adjust travel and range, follow the instructions for throttle-control adjustment above.

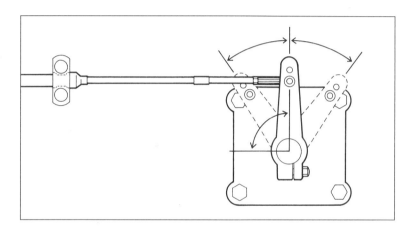

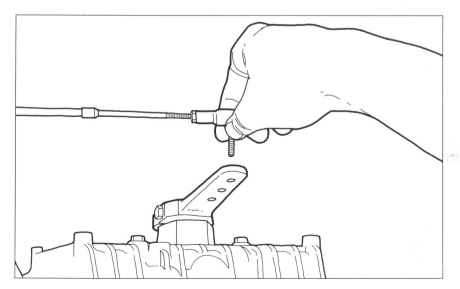

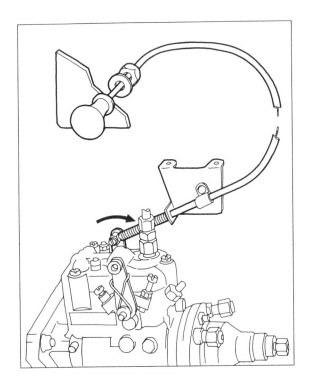

ENGINE-STOP CONTROLS

The engine-stop control cuts off the fuel supply to the injectors at the governor or injection pump and can be either mechanically or electrically operated.

Mechanical stop levers pull the shutdown arm with a cable. They require occasional lubrication, but provide reliable service and will function even when electrical power is lost.

Electrical stop controls can be either the energized-to-stop or the energized-to-run type. In energized-to-stop controls, a heavy-duty solenoid pulls the shutdown arm when the stop button is pressed. A spring returns the shutdown arm to the "run" position when power to the solenoid is cut off. If electrical power fails, it can be difficult to shut down the engine with an electrical control—particularly when the solenoid is built into the injector pump.

Many newer engines are equipped with an energized-to-run solenoid-operated valve built into the injector pump. These smaller solenoids are energized all the time the engine is running. If electrical power is cut off, the solenoid valve will close and shut down the engine fuel supply.

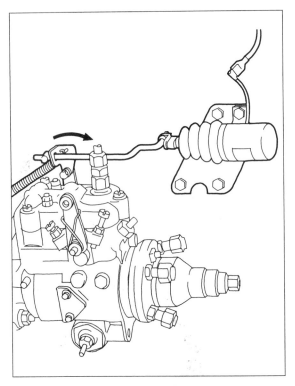

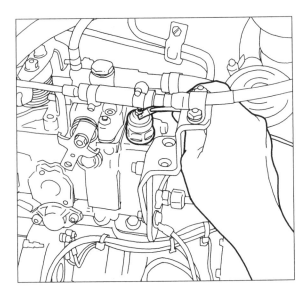

CONTROL CABLES

The control cables in throttle, gear-selector, and stop controls are normally the push-pull type with a solid stainless steel inner cable sheathed in a plastic-coated, flexible steel jacket. Such cables are very reliable, but tight turns and water ingress can lead to corrosion, splitting, and seizing.

MAINTENANCE

Lubricate the cables at the first sign of difficult movement.

If you have access to the cockpit end of the cable, disconnect the end fitting from the control lever. Rig a funnel to the jacket by attaching a small plastic bag with a strong elastic band. Fill the bag with lubricating oil and leave the cable suspended overnight. The oil will slowly work its way down the length of the cable. Operate the inner cable at full travel to speed up the process.

Alternatively, clamp a short length of hose to the jacket. Fill the hose with oil; then clamp the open end around the air hose of a bicycle pump— or better still, an electric tire-inflator pump. Gradually add air pressure to force the oil into the cable. Be careful, though: This method can be messy if you apply more pressure than your jury-rigged hose can handle.

TACHOMETERS

Mechanical tachometers are common on older engines and are very reliable. Periodically lubricate the drive cable using the method described above. Electrical tachometers are driven by signals taken from a dedicated flywheel sensor or from the alternator.

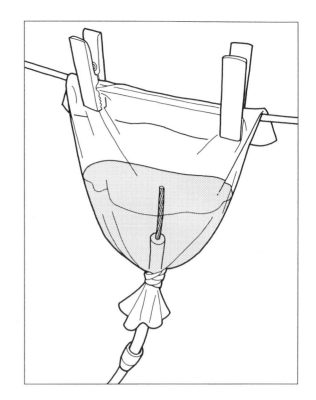

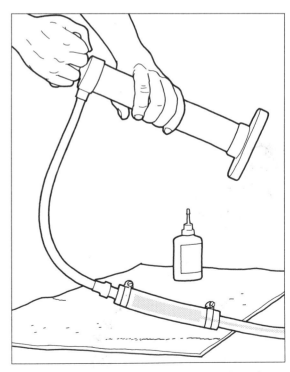

ALTERNATOR-DRIVEN TACHOMETER CONNECTIONS

Alternator-driven tachometers take their signal from the alternating current of the stator coils. Most alternators have a dedicated terminal for the tachometer output marked "R."

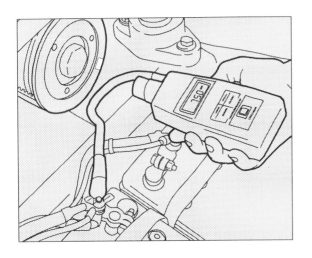

CALIBRATING TACHOMETERS

Tachometers are calibrated by the engine manufacturer and normally need no further adjustment. If you change the alternator or any of the drive pulleys, however, you must recalibrate the alternator-driven tachometer. Although this task is straightforward, you will need a phototachometer and calibration instructions for your particular tachometer; it may be easier to call in the expert for this adjustment.

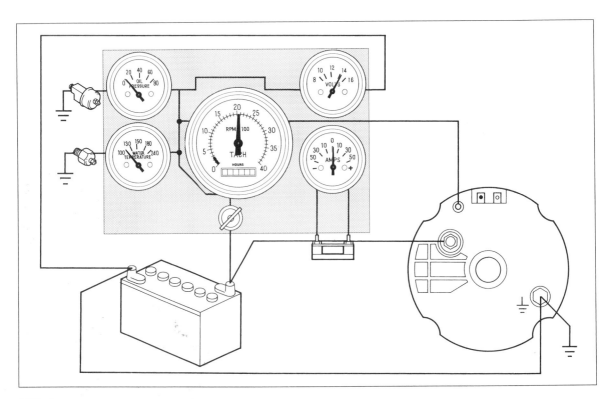

ENGINE-PANEL GAUGES

WATER TEMPERATURE

The sensor for the water-temperature gauge is usually fitted into the cylinder head close to the thermostat. On mechanical gauges, a sealed capillary tube connects a wax-filled sensor bulb to the gauge mechanism. These gauges require power only for illumination. On electrical gauges, a sender varies resistance as temperature increases.

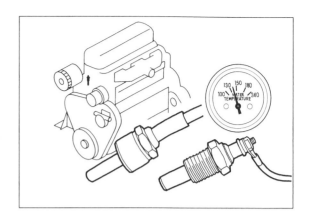

OIL PRESSURE

This gauge indicates the pressure of the lubricating oil. The pressure is usually measured just after the oil pump. Mechanical gauges use a small hose connected to the engine oil gallery. Electrical gauges use a sender fitted to the oil gallery; the sender varies resistance with changes in oil pressure.

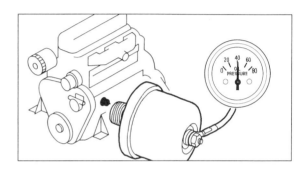

AMMETER

Control panel ammeters usually indicate alternator output. Some ammeters are connected in series and measure the current passing through the alternator output wire. Other, high-output alternators use a shunt to avoid routing heavy cables to the cockpit; this type of ammeter measures only a fraction of the current, but the gauge is calibrated to indicate the total current flow.

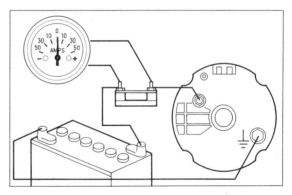

VOLTMETER

Voltmeters are connected in parallel to the circuit they measure. Most engine-panel voltmeters indicate the voltage supplied to the panel. With the ignition turned on, the meter shows the engine-starting battery voltage. Once the engine is running, the meter indicates alternator-output voltage.

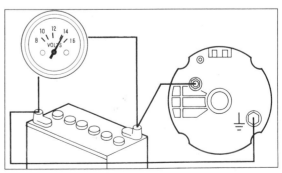

WARNING CIRCUITS

The soundproofing of a good engine installation can make it difficult to hear the onset of problems before they have caused serious and expensive damage. Oil-pressure and water-temperature gauges give excellent indication of the important engine functions but are not often installed in the most visible location. Warning circuits are an essential fail-safe that should be fitted to every marine diesel. Even the simplest design will give immediate warning of problems with oil pressure, water temperature, or charging system.

The warning circuit on a generator will automatically shut it down in the event of a problem. This may be good for the engine but could be disastrous for a boat. Warning circuits on propulsion engines should be just that—warning circuits. The decision to shut down the engine must be the helmsman's. Those extra few moments of engine power could save lives when you're heading into a rocky harbor entrance with dangerous following seas.

- A switch in the low–oil-pressure warning light circuit makes the circuit when the oil pressure drops below a preset figure. Most switches operate at around 5 psi, but such a low setting gives little time to shut down the engine before it seizes. Unless the engine normally operates at very low oil pressures, it's safer to fit a 15-psi switch that provides earlier warning.

- The high–water-temperature warning light connects to a temperature-sensitive switch in the cooling system. This switch makes the circuit when temperature rises above a preset point—usually 215°F (102°C).

- The charging warning light, commonly called the ignition light, extinguishes as soon as the alternator comes on line. The light's remaining on can be an early warning that the V-belt has failed and the engine is about to overheat.

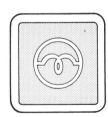

- A warning alarm is an essential piece of equipment. While you might not instantly notice a light, an alarm will get your attention. Be sure it is loud enough to be heard above engine noise and howling rigging.

If your engine does not have an alarm, rig one: A warning circuit is inexpensive and easy to install.

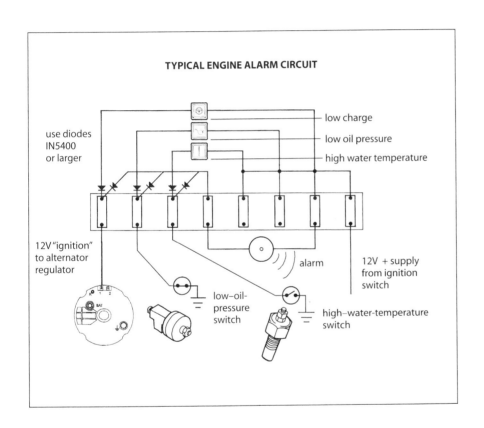

TYPICAL ENGINE ALARM CIRCUIT

— low charge

— low oil pressure

— high water temperature

use diodes
IN5400
or larger

12V "ignition"
to alternator
regulator

alarm

12V + supply
from ignition
switch

low–oil–
pressure
switch

high–water–temperature
switch

CONTROL AND INSTRUMENT FAULTS

Problem	Possible Cause	Possible Symptoms

THROTTLE CONTROL LEVER

Problem	Possible Cause	Possible Symptoms
Seized or stiff	Cable seized [2] Lever mechanism seized [2]	
Limited travel	Incorrect adjustment [2]	High idle rpm; low maximum rpm

GEAR-SELECTOR LEVER

Problem	Possible Cause	Possible Symptoms
Seized or stiff	As above	
Limited or uneven travel	As above	Poor gear selection in either or both forward and reverse

MECHANICAL STOP CONTROL

Problem	Possible Cause	Possible Symptoms
Fails to shut down engine	Cable seized [2] Lever mechanism seized [2] Cable disconnected [3] Outer sheathing not clamped correctly [3] Cable broken [4]	

ELECTRICAL STOP CONTROL—Energized to Run

Problem	Possible Cause	Possible Symptoms
Engine fails to start	Solenoid defective [4]	
Fails to shut down engine	Wiring disconnected or broken [2] Switch defective [2] Solenoid defective [4]	

ELECTRICAL STOP CONTROL—Energized to Stop

Problem	Possible Cause	Possible Symptoms
Engine fails to start	Spring return defective [3]	
Fails to shut down engine	Wiring disconnected or broken [2] Switch defective [2] Mechanical link disconnected or loose [3] Solenoid defective [4]	

TACHOMETER

Problem	Possible Cause	Possible Symptoms
No reading	Alternator defective [3] V-belt broken or thrown[3] No voltage to tachometer[4]	
Readings erratic	V-belt slipping[2] Alternator defective [3] Loose wiring[3]	Loose belt may cause overheating
Incorrect reading	Incorrect calibration [2]	

WATER-TEMPERATURE AND OIL-PRESSURE GAUGES

Problem	Possible Cause
No reading	Wiring disconnected or broken[2] Gauge defective [3] Sender defective [3] Mechanical gauge: capillary or oil-supply pipe damaged [3]
Reads in reverse	Incorrect sender [2]
Incorrect reading	Incorrect sender [2] Mechanical gauge: capillary or oil-supply pipe damaged [3]

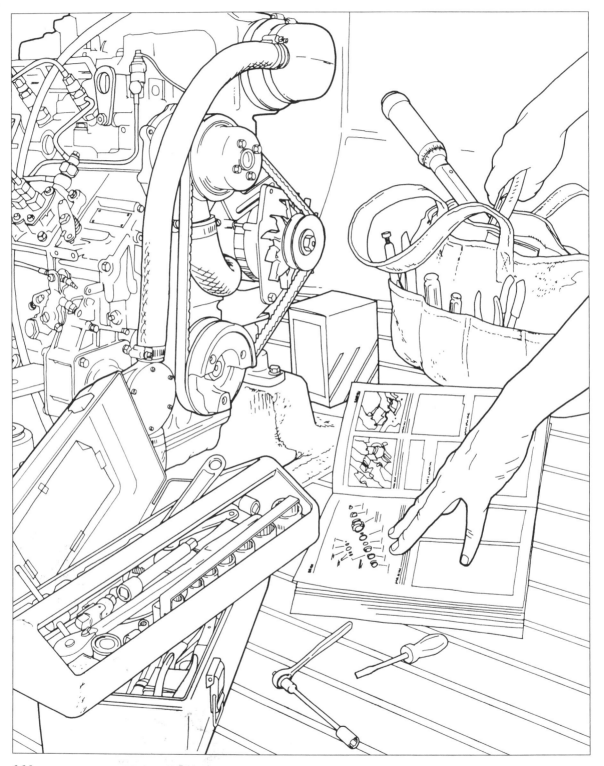

APPENDIX
DIESEL ENGINE TOOLKIT

Y ou can't do much without a set of tools. You don't need to buy the most expensive, but do buy good-quality tools: They are a pleasure to work with and will last a lifetime if you take care of them. Cheap tools break easily, and inexpensive wrenches can stretch out of shape and damage the nuts and bolts on that expensive diesel. Like any metal aboard a boat, tools are vulnerable to corrosion—especially after a few dunkings in dirty bilgewater. Wipe down your tools with a light film of oil before storing them in the toolbox for another winter.

Plastic toolboxes, unlike metal boxes, are water- and corrosion-resistant, but the cheaper varieties have weak catches that break easily with the weight of a comprehensive set of tools. Try separating tools into smaller plastic boxes that are lighter and easier to stow.

Toolbags are not waterproof, but their soft material is less likely to mark interior surfaces. Make up small cloth bags with Velcro closures to hold loose wrenches and sockets. The cloth absorbs oily fingerprints and after a while the absorbed oil builds up a protective barrier against corrosion.

A typical toolbox should include:

MECHANICAL TOOLS

- Engine repair manual
- Set of combination wrenches, $\frac{1}{4}$" – $\frac{7}{8}$"
- Set of combination wrenches, 8mm – 19mm
- Set of feeler gauges, 0.0015" – 0.025" (Unprotected, they rust very quickly, so store in a small container of oil.)
- $\frac{3}{8}$"-drive socket set, with 3/8"–1" and 10mm – 19mm sockets (Should include a ratchet handle, plus short and long extensions.)

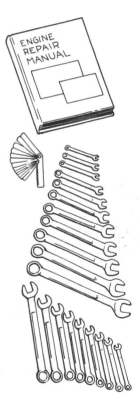

- Set of slotted screwdrivers, including a stubby
- Set of Phillips-head screwdrivers, including a stubby
- 2- or 3-lb. lump (or machinist's) hammer (It may seem large but will reduce the effort when a real hammer is needed in a confined space.)
- 1-lb. ballpeen hammer
- Set of hex (Allen) keys, standard and metric sizes
- Large and small Channel-Lock pliers
- Pair of 7" side cutters
- Medium-sized locking pliers
- Medium-sized snap-ring pliers with internal and external capability
- Adjustable wrenches, 6" and 12"
- Utility knife with spare blades
- Gasket scraper—sharp old wood chisel

ELECTRICAL TOOLS

- Digital multimeter. Don't waste money on cheap analog meters—they're pretty useless.
- Cable terminal kit including a good crimping tool (Most steel-plate crimping tools produce ineffective crimps.)
- Set of instrument (or jeweler's) screwdrivers

CRUISING TOOLS

In addition to the tools above, a cruising boat will need the following to be self-sufficient in an out-of-reach anchorage:

- Torque wrench, 30 – 100 ft. lbs.
- 12-volt or propane soldering iron and cored electrical solder
- Hacksaws, large and small
- $\frac{1}{4}$"-drive socket set, with $\frac{3}{16}$"–$\frac{1}{2}$" and 4mm –12mm sockets
- $\frac{1}{2}$"-drive socket set, with $\frac{1}{2}$"–1" (up to $1\frac{1}{2}$" if budget permits) and 10mm – 19mm sockets
- 0–6" Vernier calipers for accurate measurements
- Small propane torch
- Small and large 2- or 3-legged pullers

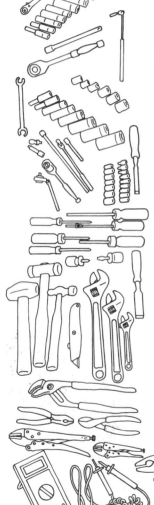

SPARE PARTS LIST

ESSENTIAL SPARES

- Raw-water pump impeller
- Raw-water pump cover-plate gasket
- Cylinder-head gasket
- Valve-cover gasket
- Oil filter(s)
- Oil
- Primary fuel filter(s)
- Secondary fuel filter(s)
- Transmission fluid
- V-belt(s)
- Coolant
- Alternator (complete)
- Assorted hose clamps

CRUISING SPARES

If you are preparing a comprehensive kit for cruising, take into account the duration of the trip and availability of spares in the region you'll be cruising. Add the following to your list of essentials.

- Raw-water pump (complete, or full overhaul kit)
- Circulating pump (complete)
- Full engine gasket set
- Full set of engine hoses
- Alternator spares, including regulator, rectifier, diode pack, and brush assembly
- Fuel lift pump
- Set of spare injectors
- Set of injector sealing washers
- Set of spare injector nozzles

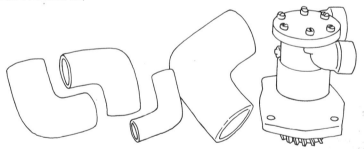

MATERIALS

SEALERS

- Oil-based instant gasket sealers, such as Permatex 2B, are excellent all-purpose sealers; they remain flexible for some time, but will harden after a few years. They are effective in just about any joint in contact with coolant, raw water, oil, or fuel.
- Silicone-based gasket sealers produce good gaskets that set quickly. Silicone is resistant to high temperatures; it tends to peel, however, and lower-quality sealers should not come in contact with fuel and oil.
- High-copper contact adhesive sprays help seal gaskets if surfaces are clean. These are useful for holding a gasket in position during assembly.
- Specialized gasket sealers such as Hylomar work well in applications requiring non-hardening properties. Hylomar is particularly effective on copper cylinder-head gaskets and resists fuel, oil, and water.

GREASES

- Silicone greases are effective on raw-water impellers, since they do not attack rubber. They also provide good protection for battery terminals.
- Lithium-based greases are waterproof; they're ideal for stuffing boxes and bearings that come into contact with water.
- Use high-temperature greases on bearings in high-speed or heavy-load applications.

CORROSION PROTECTION

- Thin, oil-based products such as WD40 are good, all-purpose corrosion inhibitors.
- Heavy-duty corrosion inhibitors such as CRC SP350 and CRC SP400 are application-specific. The latter gives effective long-term protection.

MISCELLANEOUS

- Thread-locking adhesives such as Loctite offer levels of locking according to the job.
- Antiseize compounds protect threaded components for years yet allow them to come apart when necessary.
- Penetrating fluids such as Blaster can be invaluable when you're trying to release corroded components.
- Abrasive papers should be the wet-and-dry type that will work with water and oil. Carry several grades, ranging from 100 grit to 400 grit. If any grade feels too coarse for a particular application, try rubbing it against itself to reduce its bite.

INDEX

International Marine/
Ragged Mountain Press

A Division of The **McGraw·Hill** *Companies*

Published by International Marine

10 9 8 7

Library of Congress Cataloging-in-Publication Data
Compton, Peter.
Troubleshooting Marine Diesels/Peter Compton.
   p. cm. — (International Marine sailboat library)
   Includes index.
   ISBN 0-07-012354-3 (alk. paper)
   1. Marine diesel motors—Maintenance and repair. 2. Sailboats—Maintenance and repair
   I. Title. II. Series.
   VM770.C68 1977   97-10745
   623.8'7236—dc21   CIP

Questions regarding the content of this book should be addressed to:

International Marine
P.O. Box 220
Camden, ME 04843
or
www.boatdiesel.com

Questions regarding the ordering of this book should be addressed to:

The McGraw-Hill Companies
Customer Service Department
P.O. Box 547
Blacklick, OH 43004
Retail customers: 1-800-262-4729
Bookstores: 1-800-722-4726

This book is printed on 60-pound Renew Opaque Vellum, an acid-free paper that contains 50 percent
recycled waste paper (preconsumer) and 10 percent postconsumer waste paper.

Printed by R.R. Donnelley.
Illustrations in chapters 1, 2, 4, 5, 8, 10 and on page 164 by Jim Sollers.
Illustrations in chapters 3, 6, 7, 9 and the Appendix by Rob Groves.
Illustrations on pages 8, 48, 60, 76, 94, 106, 128, 138, and 152 by Peter Compton
Design by Ann Aspell.
Production by Mary Ann Hensel and Molly Mulhern.
Edited by Jonathan Eaton; Don Casey; Mary Sullivan; Kathryn Mallien.
Cover photo courtesy of Perkins International Limited.

PETER COMPTON's dream of bluewater cruising finally became reality when, after 20 years in the Aerospace industry, he quit his job in 1986 to build a small catamaran and sail south with his family in search of sun and sand. Some 11 years and 20,000 miles later, the Comptons have settled in the British Virgin Islands. They thoroughly enjoy this civilized corner of the Caribbean.

With a background in troubleshooting that includes several years as Engineering Department Head analyzing complex system designs, Peter now applies these skills to the marine diesels he deals with every day. Although boat engines may not appear as sophisticated as the Stealth aircraft systems he helped design, Peter enjoys the practical challenge of troubleshooting diesels and can often be found covered in oil, squeezed into an engine bay.

Peter's current project is an independent and informative website that covers every aspect of marine diesels. Visit it at www.boatdiesel.com.

THE INTERNATIONAL MARINE SAILBOAT LIBRARY

Troubleshooting Marine Diesels has company:

Sailboat Refinishing
by Don Casey
Hardcover, 144 pages, 350 illustrations, $21.95. Item No. 0-07-013225-9

Sailboat Hull & Deck Repair
by Don Casey
Hardcover, 144 pages, 350 illustrations, $21.95. Item No. 0-07-013369-7

Canvaswork & Sail Repair
by Don Casey
Hardcover, 144 pages, 350 illustrations, $21.95. Item No. 0-07-013391-3

Inspecting the Aging Sailboat
by Don Casey
Hardcover, 144 pages, 300 illustrations, $21.95. Item No. 0-07-013394-8

The Sailor's Assistant: Reference Data for Maintenance, Repair, & Cruising
by John Vigor
Hardcover, 176 pages, 140 illustrations, $21.95. Item No. 0-07-067476-0

Sailboat Electrics Simplified
by Don Casey
Hardcover, 160 pages, 320 illustrations, $21.95. Item No. 0-07-036649-7

100 Fast and Easy Boat Improvements
by Don Casey
Hardcover, 144 pages, 200 illustrations, $21.95. Item No. 0-07-013402-2

Boatowner's Weekend Woodworking
by Garth Graves
Hardcover, 144 pages, 200 illustrations, $21.95. Item No. 0-07-024696-3

"This is the most helpful guide to marine diesel engines I've seen, and should be especially useful to nonmechanically inclined boatowners. The clearly illustrated and prioritized troubleshooting charts are a godsend. Most people tend to 'over-troubleshoot,' and they wind up missing a simple, easily remedied problem because they're looking for something bigger. Compton lists malfunctions in order of their likelihood, which is brilliant. Just follow the numbers, refer to the illustrations, and let the book work for you. I'm delighted to have this book in the shop."
—Michael Muessel, President, Oldport Marine Services, Inc., Newport, RI